I HAVE A PROBLEM

how to solve any problem, any time

by Ellen L. Glatstein

Second Edition

Copyright © Ellen Glatstein, 2016

All Rights Reserved

Second Edition

Printed in the United States of America

Cover design by Rachel Maya Fremeth

No part of this publication may be reproduced, stored in or introduced into a retrieval system, or transmitted, in any form, or by any means (electronic, mechanical, photocopying, recording or otherwise) without the prior written permission of the copyright owner.

All requests for permission to reproduce material from this work should be directed to Idea Greenhouse, LLC, at www.idea-greenhouse.com.

For Scott, who makes my world better every day.

TABLE OF CONTENTS

Introduction   9

Section I: Creative Problem Solving Background   15

Chapter 1	Creative Problem Solving	17
Chapter 2	Open Mindset	23
Chapter 3	Creative Thinking Styles	29
Chapter 4	Greenhouse Thinking™	38
Chapter 5	Breaking Assumptions	46

Section II: The CPS Process   57

Chapter 6	The Right Problem	59
Chapter 7	Wishing	66
Chapter 8	Strategic Territory	73
Chapter 9	Excursion Theory	79
Chapter 10	Excursion Tools	89
Chapter 11	Setting Criteria	129
Chapter 12	Selecting Ideas	138
Chapter 13	Developing Lead Ideas	152
Chapter 14	Quality Check	168

Section III: Tips & Guidelines to Ensure Success 175

Chapter 15	Planning the Meeting	177
Chapter 16	Creating the Ideal Team	186
Chapter 17	In-Meeting Tips	194
Chapter 18	Group Dynamics	209
Chapter 19	Doing it All Yourself	219
Chapter 20	Culture of Innovation	230

Conclusion   **240**

Index   **243**

INTRODUCTION

Do you have a problem? Of course you do! Everyone does, all the time--it's part of life. But what if you had a simple and easy-to-use tool to solve all your problems? Any problem, any time, no matter the context, the complexity or the amount of frustration it has caused. One by one, we would use this tool to solve every problem as it arises, to improve our lives in small or big ways and make the world a better place, not only for ourselves but for everyone around us as well.

Sound too good to be true? It's not! But it does require a process—because creative solutions don't just pop into people's heads whenever a problem exists in their lives. Finding the solution takes Creative Problem Solving (CPS), a technique trademarked by Alex Osborn and Sidney Parnes in the 1960s to describe a process that helps people use brainstorming to break down problems and build them back up into solutions.

Since then, many other variations of the Creative Problem Solving process have been used to solve hundreds of thousands of business and personal problems. The process always works, and it will work for you.

Better yet, this book shows you how to do it all—how to identify the right problem, generate ideas, evaluate those ideas, create an action plan and implement the plan until the problem is solved.

MY BACKGROUND

The information in this book is the culmination of a 25-year career (so far!) in creative problem solving and business innovation. As a child with some artistic ability, I was always in love with anything creative, starting with making homemade greeting cards at age six and adding my logo "Home Made Card Company" to each one. All kinds of creative classes soon followed, including dance, drawing, oil painting, sculpture, macramé (it was the 70s after all), stained glass, piano lessons, singing, cross stitching, needlepoint, you name it. I loved them all.

As I grew older, I dreamed of opening a creative business of my own someday. But I put that aside to be "practical" and "make a decent living"—I decided to keep my creative pursuits as a hobby while I pursued an MBA.

Then, by some fluke I came across a Procter & Gamble recruiting brochure which described an incredibly fun brand management job that would make me the "hub of the wheel" within a cross-functional team. I pursued the opportunity, was offered a job in brand management at both Procter & Gamble and General Mills, and ultimately chose to join General Mills and move to Minneapolis.

At General Mills I worked on several brand teams, including Gold Medal Flour, Nature Valley Granola Bars, Golden Grahams and new packaged dinners; and I quickly discovered that the real fun, for me at least, happened whenever I was involved with new innovation and future vision work. At last I had found my niche!

A few years later, I moved on to Ralston Purina in St. Louis to manage Purina Canned Cat Food. A year later I was assigned to new product innovation, where we began conducting brainstorming sessions to address all kinds of challenges: systemic cost savings, new product ideas, new promotion opportunities and much more. I loved leading the sessions, and I loved building concepts from the new ideas afterwards even more.

CREDIT WHERE CREDIT IS DUE

After taking a couple of years off to have babies I joined a company in Minneapolis known then as Fred Meyer Associates. Fred Meyer had a successful career at Campbell Mithun Advertising and had worked on CPS within the agency for several years when he decided to strike out on his own. Fred started his own innovation firm that facilitated creative problem solving from a unique perspective — the consumer's perspective. He hired me in 1993, and over the next ten years I helped his firm build best practices while developing my own book of business.

Needless to say, Fred taught me *almost* everything I know. Eventually he changed the name of his company to Ideas to Go, and several years later he sold it and retired. In 2003 I left Ideas to Go to start my own company, Idea Greenhouse, which now competes with Ideas to Go and other firms that have cropped up over the years to fill this space. In 2016 we opened a kid-client co-creation arm of our company, called Idea Playhouse, formalizing the work with children we had been doing for the past 10 years.

All of the best practices described in this book came from my cumulative CPS experience, which incorporates what I've learned from many sources, including: Fred Meyer; Synectics Training; Osborne-Parnes Creative Problem Solving; Roger Van Oeck and his "Creative Whack Pack"; the International Creative Problem Solving Institute; years of reading books and articles about the creative mind; and the many, many client projects I have completed across dozens of categories with a wide range of companies and corporate cultures.

THE PROCESSES WE USE AT IDEA GREENHOUSE

All of the innovation work we do focuses on consumer co-creation, where clients and their target consumers work side by side solving problems together. Idea Greenhouse utilizes adult ConsumerVisionaries™--bright and imaginative mainstream consumers who naturally think laterally. Idea Playhouse utilizes KidVisionaries™ --kids and teens who naturally think laterally.

Resulting ideas meet the needs of consumers—the end users of the product or service—while meeting the strategic needs of the company at the same time. To accommodate the severe time demands our clients face we've streamlined the process to be focused, fast and efficient. To maintain research rigor we complete all the key steps but compress them into tight, highly efficient blocks. This enables us to get more done in less time, with minimal use of client resources.

A typical schedule looks like this:

- Day One: Consumer-Client Co-creation
  - Clients work side by side (or online) with consumers to generate lots and lots of ideas.

- At the end of the day consumers leave and clients set criteria and click-vote on those ideas that meet the criteria.
- Electronic vote-ranking plus championed ideas determine the set of lead ideas.
- We write and illustrate concepts overnight.

- Day Two: Concept Editing and Iterative Representative Focus Groups
- The client edits and finalizes concepts early Day Two.
  - Our moderator conducts Focus Group #1, designed to generate reactions, likes, dislikes and favorite/least favorite selection.
  - Our writer uses learning to revise concepts.
  - Our moderator conducts Focus Group #2 with revised concepts.
  - Our writer uses learning to revise concepts.
  - Our moderator conducts Focus Group #3 with re-revised concepts.

- Day Three: Half-day Debrief
  - We discuss general learning from the complete process with the client.
  - Together, we identify concept-specific learning and actions.
  - The team determines next steps.
  - We rewrite/re-illustrate concepts in quantitative test format.

Bottom line: The processes shared in this book will help you break through really tough problems to find great, innovative and practical solutions. Whether you are working alone to solve a personal problem or working on a team to solve a business problem, this book gives you the resources to do it yourself like a pro.

Each chapter explores a different aspect of our streamlined CPS process with simple-to-follow techniques you can apply any time to make your corner of the world a slightly better place. Both personal problem solving and business problem solving are addressed allowing you to use these best practices in many different ways.

Business problem solving principles are explained using concrete, real-world examples; at the end of each chapter you will find a Chapter Summary that provides you with everything at a glance, plus tips for both personal and business problem solving.

Let's start creating!!

IMPORTANT NOTE

Due to our confidentiality commitments, all of the anecdotes, example business problems, solutions, concepts, ideas and client companies listed in this book are *fictionalized* versions of a real event or project. The issues are accurate but all the specific details have been changed to protect corporate secrets.

SECTION I:
CREATIVE PROBLEM SOLVING BACKGROUND

CHAPTER ONE

WHAT IS CREATIVE PROBLEM SOLVING?

WHAT IS CREATIVE PROBLEM SOLVING?

Creative Problem Solving, or CPS, is a deliberate process originally designed to assist researchers in finding solutions to the many problems they faced. The process is based on two key principles:

1. A diversity of perspectives from many will yield a more comprehensive list of possible solutions than one person could create on his/her own.

2. A quantity of ideas is more likely to uncover quality solutions than working with just a few ideas.

The developers of CPS believed that working with a diverse group of people would generate a large number of possible solutions to a problem, from which a "best" solution could be identified more quickly and easily than from the fact-based approaches favored at the time.

CPS involves two distinct steps: 1) Generate and record a large number of solutions to the problem without judgment—this is called divergence; 2) then set criteria and select the best solution—this step is known as convergence.

A BRIEF HISTORY OF CPS

In the 1920s, an adman named Alex Osborn joined a Buffalo, NY firm that would later be known as Batten, Barton, Durstine and Osborne (BBD&O). Widely known for coining the term "brainstorming," Osborn had an interest in creativity from the very beginning and in 1952 published his first book on the subject, *Wake Up Your Mind: 101 Ways to Develop Creativeness.* He also believed that creativity could be taught and, in 1954, shared his methodology with others by forming the Creative Education Foundation and the Creative Problem Solving Institute at Buffalo State College.

In 1964 he wrote a second book, *Your Creative Power: How to Use Imagination,* which was followed by a third book, *How to Become More Creative.* Both books build on the principles of creativity and offer ways to become more conscious of the creative power within everyone's reach. Osborne argues that all human beings have the ability to be creative; what's required is accessing the ability deliberately.

From this base of knowledge Osborn developed a process to assist those for whom creativity does not come naturally. This process involved three distinct stages of diverging and converging: Fact Finding, Idea Finding and Solution Finding.

ENTER SIDNEY PARNES

Parnes joined Osborn in 1955 at the first Creative Problem Solving Institute conference, and together they developed the Osborn-Parnes Creative Problem Solving process as we know it today. A PhD psychologist, Sidney Parnes became a professor at Buffalo State College and in 1956 began working alongside Osborn as co-founder of the International Center for Studies in Creativity. Osborn and Parnes shared a passion for helping people release their creative potential on both professional and personal levels, which made them natural collaborators. Although Osborn had already created the idea, it was Parnes who developed and organized it into a methodology that could be taught to anyone, to help achieve an ultimate goal. Together, Osborn and Parnes aimed to help the world unlock its creative potential.

When Osborn died in 1967, Sidney Parnes—who was significantly younger—would continue their legacy by teaching the model in five continents, speaking at hundreds of conferences and seminars and publishing over a dozen books.

So what exactly is this Creative Problem Solving process or CPS as it is often called? The Osborn-Parnes CPS model has a basic structure comprised of four stages:

1. Clarify: Identify the territory and select the right problem statement to solve.
2. Ideate: Create many ideas and select those with the greatest potential for solving the problem.
3. Develop: Take the best idea options and elaborate on them to optimize them into a small number of clear solutions.
4. Implement: Create concrete action plans for the best solution(s).

Within each of these four steps, two distinct types of thinking are used sequentially: divergent thinking first, to create dozens of possible options, followed by convergent thinking to arrive at one best solution.

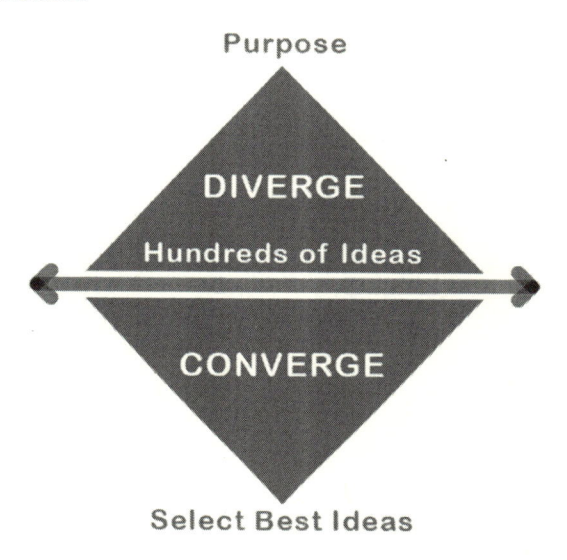

Purpose

DIVERGE
Hundreds of Ideas

CONVERGE

Select Best Ideas

This book outlines a simple, more streamlined approach to CPS—one that has been developed and perfected over time to quickly and effectively address both business and personal problems.

INNOVATION VERSUS PROBLEM SOLVING

We often hear the question, "What is the difference between innovation and creative problem solving?" My answer: It's simply a question of scope. Creative Problem Solving is a process designed to tackle any issue—literally anything! Creating new innovations is simply one issue to address using CPS.

For example, if we think in terms of "how to [accomplish some goal]," Creative Problem Solving could easily address:

- How to prevent spilling on my shirt at lunch
- How to avoid family conflict at homework time
- How to get my kids to put their dirty clothes in the hamper
- How to get my holiday baking done in half the time
- How to find a fun new place to vacation
- How to get a healthful dinner on the table in 20 minutes five nights a week
- How to revolutionize transportation to achieve zero carbon emissions
- How to unify all cultures and create world peace

In the business world, CPS can easily address any business problem, too:

- How to grow my business via new products or services
- How to reduce costs on our XYZ production line
- How to increase retail distribution without large trade budgets
- How to identify new prospective customers to target
- Etc.

But before going further, let's give a quick thanks to Alex Osborn and Sidney Parnes for the gift they have given us: the ability to unlock any roadblock and solve any problem in our lives.

CHAPTER ONE SUMMARY – THE CPS PROCESS

1. Creative Problem Solving is a process born out of Osborn's "brainstorming" and embellished by Parnes to create a deliberate method.

2. All Creative Problem Solving involves two separate but equal steps: diverging to create many possible solutions, followed by converging in which the best solutions are selected.

3. CPS is a universal problem-solving process; using it to create innovations is simply one issue CPS can address.

TIPS FOR PERSONAL PROBLEM SOLVING

1. Adhere to the two distinct steps; do not be tempted to evaluate while you are generating options.

2. The process works—every time. Trust it and follow it.

TIPS FOR BUSINESS PROBLEM SOLVING

1. Set clear expectations for your team up front so they understand that CPS is a two-stage process, and that you are asking them to suspend judgment during the first stage for a very good reason.

2. At times you may need to remind your team to "trust the process," because business people who love to think critically and analyze options may be tempted to evaluate and edit ideas prematurely.

CHAPTER TWO

THE IMPORTANCE OF KEEPING AN OPEN MINDSET

This chapter outlines a MINDSET to start you on your way to solving every problem you encounter—business or personal. Think of it as the rules of engagement—it's important to enter this process with a clear understanding of guidelines in order to emerge successful in the end.

It all starts with a few rules of thinking:

1. **Always think about what you DO want rather than what you DON'T want.**

   - For example, instead of saying "I wish I weren't crushed by debt," it's much more powerful to think "I wish I had abundant funds at all times."

   - It's easy to focus on the negative since you've already identified that there's a problem—a huge, invasive, stress-inducing problem. So it's natural that your mind would be swimming with all the barriers and negative elements holding you back. It's especially easy to identify all the things you don't want because those are just smaller problems that contribute to the larger one. "I don't want bill collectors calling me every week," and "I don't want my entire paycheck to go to bills each month" represent only a piece of the larger issue, which is how to have abundant funds at all times.

- So we ask you to work just a little harder. Of course you don't want to be crushed by debt or pestered by bill collectors, but dwelling on problems won't get you closer to the solution. That's a passive approach which takes you two steps back instead of moving you forward.

- Instead we ask you to adjust your thinking to focus on the positive. If you identify what you DO want you're setting a direction, defining a goal and establishing a destination to work towards. And that immediately moves you to the next step—how to achieve what you DO want.

- Once you've left the negative behind you can begin the process with a clear direction leading toward your solution. And that brings us to our next guideline.

2. **Look FORWARD to what could be; do not look BACK at "what is."**

    - Managers often like to examine history to find a new future. And it's true: by looking at the past they can see every product that was created, tested and released. They can see what was successful and what failed, which ideas were brilliant and which ideas flopped. However, just like wallowing in negativity, the more we immerse ourselves in what is and what has been, the harder it is to create what could be. We get trapped in the box and become instantly limited by the hundreds or thousands of ideas that have already been considered.

- Think about it: We wouldn't examine old technology to find new technology, because the old technology solved a PAST problem and it takes new technology to solve a future problem. For example, what good is examining the 8 Track, the compact cassette tape and even CDs, when the world has moved on from all of those to streaming music? In other words, it's not about where we've been but where we're going next.

- Instead of revisiting the past, examine the "probable" or "possible" future to anticipate what is coming and create a current and relevant solution. To do this you have to forget not only what you know, but also what you've seen and where you've been. You must think only about where you're going and what your needs are, both now and in the future. Those who think in such a context have created some of the world's most memorable contributions. And the solution to your problem is no different.

3. **Ignore your competitors while inventing; borrow ideas from other "worlds" instead.**

    - This might seem counterintuitive, so let me explain. It's tempting to focus on competition when innovating, but the more we focus on the "reality" of what your industry is doing the harder it is to create something useful and NEW. What good does it really do to create a "me too" product? Repeating something that already exists gives you very little competitive advantage in the marketplace. In fact, by borrowing ideas from your competitors you're creating

25

Band-Aids for your problems, or short-term fixes that may or may not be sustainable longer term.

- For example, it's severely limiting to examine competitors' cars to find innovations for a new one; again, it's much more powerful to borrow ideas from other worlds your consumer or end user lives in, and then apply them to cars. You might begin by looking at lifestyle trends to help identify the needs of your end user. For example, in trying to improve the sport utility vehicle, you can ask yourself, "what is the typical day like for a single mother of four as it relates to her car? Where is her family going, and what are they doing?" You could also look at other "family spaces," such as open concept homes that bring people together to help design the car interior of the future.

- Once you've identified those elements you can apply them to your own product in order to create something that fits into the user's lifestyle. Continuing with this SUV example, you could think about new car features to help with dinner on the run; or create features that make it comfortable for families to "live in the car" as they constantly run from one activity to the next.

Bottom line: Before you can solve anything, you have to adjust your mindset. A closed mind—focused on all the negatives, focused on the past and focused on the work of everyone else—will keep you rooted in your challenge and keep you from reaching your goals.

By contrast, changing your thinking will change your future. And changing the way you view your problem will take you miles further in solving it. You'll be amazed by how powerful this simple shift can be.

CHAPTER TWO SUMMARY – KEEPING A POSITIVE MINDSET

- Think in terms of what you DO want, not what you DON'T want.

- Look forward to what could be, not back at what has been.

- Go outside your topic or industry and borrow user-centric ideas to apply to your problem.

TIPS FOR PERSONAL PROBLEM SOLVING

1. It can be hard to think positively about personal problems because we tend to think first of what we don't want. If you have difficulty doing this, write down a "whining" list of your problems before you begin. Then, systematically turn each negative into its positive.

2. As you look at what could be don't mire yourself in assumptions and constraints. Push it all aside and create an ideal world scenario for your perfect future that you can work toward.

3. As you look "outside" for solutions, think about parallel problems that may provide rich fodder for solutions. For example, a problem with weight loss probably has a lot in common with behavioral changes like the need to quit smoking or begin flossing, to name a few of many self-help or self-improvement topics that can be explored.

TIPS FOR BUSINESS PROBLEM SOLVING

1. The more knowledge a person has of an industry or product, the harder it is to view business issues from 40,000 feet. Consider stakeholder research, including end user research to help you identify what you want.

2. Business analysis, by its very nature, focuses exclusively on the past. It is a strong and helpful tool when used at the right time to report "what is" based on the past as well as the current state of affairs. Conduct your analysis as background information to help you identify key issues. Then, look at each issue and use future thinking to identify opportunities for "what could be."

CHAPTER THREE

CREATIVE THINKING STYLES: LINEAR THINKING VS. LATERAL THINKING

Before we embark on brainstorming, a few words about linear vs. lateral thinkers would be helpful. This chapter outlines the definition of each thinking style, the behaviors the two types of thinkers tend to exhibit and how to use different thinking styles to yield maximum results.

Most of the American population thinks in a LINEAR way, and this is especially true of successful business people. Linear thinking is highly organized, sequential and bound by logic: If A = B and B = C, then A = C. Linear thinkers like organizing their thoughts within a framework whether it's chronological, prioritized or logical-sequential. Most successful business people are great at financial analysis, budgeting, efficient logistics, lean operations and many other highly organized and highly detailed business disciplines. They often prefer working with facts and data vs. "soft and squishy" issues.

By contrast, lateral thinkers naturally use a more indirect, nonlinear approach. If you listen carefully to lateral thinkers, you will find they often use analogies or, in this case, a metaphor to describe a situation: "That meeting was a train wreck!" Another great example of lateral thinking occurred during a brainstorming session designed to generate ideas about new fun snacks for kids. Here's an excerpt from that discussion:

"This marker smells like cinnamon which reminds me of the oatmeal cookies my mom used to make for my brother, but I didn't like them which reminds me of the kind of cookies I liked which were chocolate chip cookies, and she would sometimes surprise us after school with a fresh batch. That makes me think of 'Chocolate Chip Surprises' snacks, which are high fiber, high protein cupcakes with chocolate chip "surprises" hidden in the center."

This idea started with a cinnamon-scented marker and ended up with a fun snack idea for kids. As demonstrated above, a lateral thinker can jump from one thought to another, seemingly at random, and then tie it back to the issue. Lateral thinkers are not universally loved within the business world because they can come off as "random" or "scattered." In truth, they are simply unbound by the logical and sequential constraints their teammates may experience.

KIRTON ADAPTION–INNOVATION INVENTORY

The distinction between linear and lateral thinking has been studied in depth by Dr. M.J. Kirton, who developed the KAI—a self-reported inventory tool that measures a person's creative style. Many students of creativity ask "How creative am I?" This question assumes that creativity is a limited "quantity" of some kind, and that some of us are blessed with a lot while others have none at all. Under this assumption some people are truly "creative," while others are labeled as being "not creative."

By asking a different question—"How am I creative?"—Dr. Kirton focuses on the different ways people express creativity. He argues that we have all been pre-programmed to solve problems creatively every day as a basic survival skill. For example, when we're hiking on a path and find it blocked with a fallen tree we are programmed to find a way over or through it. This creative process takes place in our brains every minute of every day.

Dr. Kirton labels and describes the two distinct styles as: 1) "adaptive creativity," or building incrementally to optimize others' ideas and 2) "innovative creativity," which is creating ideas completely out of context. And he uses a bell curve to show that while some individuals fall on the more extreme ends, the vast majority of us fall somewhere in the middle.

When I began using KAI in the business world I soon discovered that the term "Innovative" can be highly value-laden for many. Who wouldn't wish to be known as "innovative" versus "merely adaptive," especially when, according to Dr. Kirton's scoring tool, a lower score of <100 means you're adaptive, while a higher score of 100+ means you're innovative. Value-laden labels and low numbers simply don't feel very good to the adapters, even though the intent of the tool is to show that styles are different and neither one is better than the other.

To make sure all participants can feel proud of their creative style, as Dr. Kirton intended, I use the KAI tool with different labels and scoring.

My term for adaptive creativity is the "linear/Thomas Edison" style which creates in a systematic way. We all know Thomas

Edison made several real-world inventions that truly work—the light bulb, the phonograph, the movie camera and much more. To create these devices Mr. Edison conducted hundreds of experiments in a highly structured way, adjusting only one variable each time until he found the right combination to make the device work.

When asked to create new ideas Thomas Edison thinkers will come up with one or two ideas and feel that's more than enough to consider. And if you don't like their ideas they may take offense, as they took great care to come up with what they believe are the best possible solutions.

On the other end of the curve are those who naturally use Dr. Kirton's innovative creativity style to pull lots of wild ideas out of thin air—I refer to them as "lateral/DaVinci" thinkers. Leonardo DaVinci created hundreds of inventions and sketched them up on paper but never felt a need to take most of them further. His inventions include the first helicopter, the first airplane, air conditioning, the first self-propelled vehicle, the parachute, the machine gun and much more. It was hundreds of years before anyone began working to bring some of his inventions to life in the real world. But people like DaVinci would have no interest in making the ideas real—they would much prefer to keep thinking of new ideas than tackle the tedious job of making the invention actually work.

In contrast to Edison thinkers, DaVinci thinkers prefer to come up with dozens and dozens of ideas. And they don't care whether you like the idea they just suggested because they have literally dozens more waiting in the wings.

REAL WORLD APPLICATION

Now let's apply Dr. Kirton's thinking to the business world. Because most successful business people are linear thinkers and their organized thinking is such a critical factor in their success, they may be uncomfortable working with lateral thinkers who can seem disorganized and scattered.

When it comes to innovation, linear/Edison thinkers prefer to innovate within context because that's what they know best and their search is fact-based. For example, I had one client who was looking to grow the company's business with a new line of snacks containing nuts. To find a new idea, the team searched for everything that exists in the world with nuts as an ingredient. Can you imagine how many examples emerged from that search? Now imagine looking at that list to try and create something that is NOT yet invented. That, I can tell you, is nearly impossible even for the wildest, craziest thinkers.

While searching for new ideas within context can work very well for incremental improvements, the approach falls short when you're looking for new innovations that cannot be easily copied by all your competitors.

Lateral/DaVinci thinkers prefer to innovate outside of context. When looking for a new idea for a snack with nuts, for example, they will study restaurant trends involving nuts, nutritional trends and "power foods" research, snack products containing seeds but not nuts, high protein innovations in food products, food with a sweet and savory flavor combo, appetizer ideas with nuts that can be adapted to be a snack, etc. This approach can be much more effective when true innovation is the goal.

The real power, however, lies in combining the two styles. Here's how that works: First, the DaVinci participant throws out a wild idea that fits the challenge. Then the Thomas Edison participants build on the idea to make it realistic. Both ideas — the wild one and the build-- are captured to create a stronger result.

To use a familiar hockey metaphor, the lateral thinker provides the assist to the goal and the linear thinker slaps the shot in to make the score. This approach is perfect for the business world which loves nothing better than a brand new, unique idea that's completely realistic and feasible. Combining thinking styles in your brainstorming session will help you find truly breakthrough, real world options.

It's also helpful to understand how the two types of thinkers view one another. It's not surprising that linear thinkers tend to believe that lateral thinkers are flaky, misguided dreamers who prefer fantasy, tangents and playing with irrelevant, vague concepts. Lateral thinkers tend to believe their counterparts are unimaginative, constrained, rigid and sadly limited realists, who are too tied to practicality and feasibility to ever come up with anything new. Of course, neither characterization represents the truth, and both groups significantly benefit from collaboration.

CHAPTER THREE SUMMARY – EMBRACING YOUR THINKING STYLE.

1. We are all creative; we just have different creative styles. The question is not "How creative am I?" but rather "How am I creative?"

2. There are two distinct creative-thinking styles: linear thinking (logic) and lateral thinking (thinking in analogies and metaphors).

3. Linear or "Thomas Edison" thinkers:
   - Are detail-oriented.
   - Think in a systematic way.
   - Prefer to create variations on an existing idea than to invent totally new-to-the-world ideas.
   - Prefer to work in context to find new ideas.
   - Are great at suggesting incremental improvements that make wild ideas real.
   - Prefer to suggest only one or two ideas, and enjoy the execution phase.
   - Represent about 90% of the American population.

4. Lateral or "DaVinci" thinkers:
   - Prefer to think in big picture "generalities."
   - Often use analogy and metaphor to describe what they experience.
   - Think in a more randomized way.
   - Prefer to create new-to-the-world ideas.
   - Tend to work outside of context to "borrow" ideas from other realms to apply to the problem.
   - Are great at suggesting big, sweeping changes.
   - Prefer generating dozens and dozens of ideas and leaving the execution to someone else.

- Represent only about 7-10% of the American population.

5. Both thinking styles are very important to brainstorming. A lateral/DaVinci thinker may come up with a wild and impractical starting idea; then the linear/Edison thinker builds on the idea to make it logical, practical and new — the holy grail of brainstorming!!

TIPS FOR PERSONAL PROBLEM SOLVING

1. If you are working alone you obviously have only one thinking style to utilize — your own. Try to identify which style best describes you.

2. Once you have an idea of your thinking style re-read the sections above to understand your style's strengths and weaknesses.

3. If you are a natural linear thinker, push yourself to consider other perspectives on the problem, to create many more ideas than you normally would and to suspend judgement so you can stretch yourself to uncover several worthwhile and new ideas.

4. If you are a natural lateral thinker, push yourself to develop your ideas into more detailed thoughts, focus on building on a single idea to make it realistic, and know when to stop coming up with new options in order to begin converging on the best options.

TIPS FOR BUSINESS PROBLEM SOLVING

1. If you can afford the time and small expense, consider giving your brainstorming team a creative style assessment, so team members understand their own thinking styles and how to work productively with those of a different thinking style.

2. If you cannot administer an assessment, do your best to assess your potential team members' thinking styles when you plan your brainstorming session.

3. Strive for a mix of thinking styles to take advantage of the natural tag-team approach—get a starter idea from a DaVinci thinker and invite Edison thinkers to build on the idea long enough to make it realistic.

4. Remember that whatever your thinking style, you may be uncomfortable working with people who use the opposite style. Know they are experiencing the same thing as they work with you and your style.

CHAPTER FOUR

GREENHOUSE THINKING™: CARE AND HANDLING OF FLEDGLING IDEAS

Now that we've discussed Mindset and Thinking Styles, we can address how to protect and nurture those brand new ideas. The approach presented here ties directly to the positive thinking we discussed in Chapter Two, and offers a concrete technique to grow seedling ideas into towering oaks. (Yes, I am a metaphorical thinker! Did you note the analogy here?)

Our technique is based on a positive-thinking process I learned from Fred Meyer.

CPS saves evaluating ideas for the second step, so it's important to suspend judgment during step one as you generate ideas. While that sounds easy, it's the "no judgment" part that's hard.

We've all been to painful meetings that began with the intent to share ideas. Consider this example. On the following page is a picture of a 'new idea' that's still rough around the edges—it contains good aspects, negatives and even some vagueness. When someone shares an imperfect idea like this one, somehow the focus quickly turns to the negative and what won't work with little if any discussion on the merit within the idea. We hear comments like "That's stupid" or "It costs too much" or

"We tried that before," and the list goes on. Unfortunately, negative reactions crush the spirit of teammates and create a poor environment for idea proliferation.

The result? We share only safe ideas or shut down altogether and contribute nothing. Who wants to sign up for that kind of abuse?

We've been taught to think critically since elementary school, so it's hard to shut off our internal "Yes, but," especially when it comes to our own ideas. We have been carefully taught for example, that it's "wrong" to color an elephant purple, but it's "right" to color it gray. From Kindergarten on we learn to edit ourselves and our ideas to conform to the world's expectations.

To break the habit create a "Greenhouse Environment."

A greenhouse is an enclosed, protected, bright and warm space that grows things. As such, it's the perfect metaphor for the confidential, protected environment and mindset in which ideas can grow. To create this environment, use the Greenhouse Thinking™ technique:

1. First, write down everything you LIKE about a new idea.

39

2. Then instead of writing down everything you dislike, like a pros and cons list, we ask you to write down what you WISH FOR to overcome what you dislike.

It may look something like this:

LIKES	WISHES

For example, an in-store promotion idea may "cost too much." To work with this idea instead of killing it off, begin by listing what's good about the in-store promotion, what's working, what you can build on and what will move you closer to your end goal.

LIKES

- Likely to attract our desired target audience
- Increases consumer awareness of our product
- Increases store traffic for our retail partners
- Is fun, engaging, and memorable

Next, list wishes that *overcome* what you don't like in the idea. For the example above, wishes to overcome the cost issue might include:

WISHES

- I wish to partner with non-competitors to share costs.
- I wish to hire summer interns to execute affordably.
- I wish to source supplies in China.
- I wish to build so much value into the idea that our retail partners want to contribute their own money to the endeavor.
- I wish it would be so fun and engaging that consumers are happy to pay more.

This technique allows us to bypass time-wasting discussions of the problems and what won't work, and go right to possible solutions.

As you are generating wishes allow yourself to mold or change the idea to make it more practical. Or add a wish to build additional features that make it more practical.

Using an example from the promotion above, the statement, "I wish it would be so fun and engaging that consumers are happy to pay more" mitigates the issue of cutting costs and offers another solution that reflects a completely different perspective from all the others.

BENEFITS OF GREENHOUSE THINKING™

1. **The technique identifies the good in an idea and keeps it alive.** In the above example every "like" is a starting point for new ideas: "How else might we increase consumer awareness" or "What else is engaging to our target?"

Dozens of "FUN" promotion ideas

Other promos that increase consumer awareness

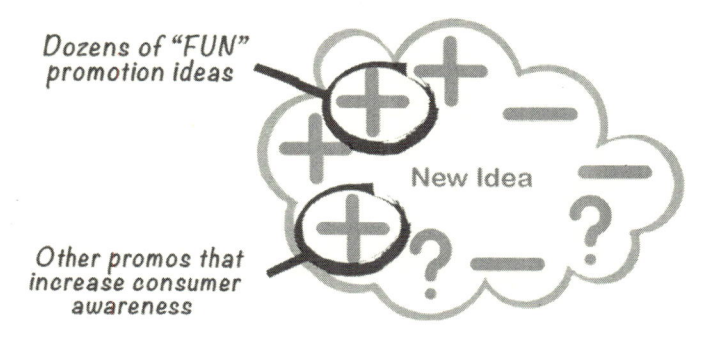

New Idea

2. **Thinking this way steers the idea toward practicality.** By wishing we are able to add, take away or change anything to improve the idea and make it work in the real world.

New Idea

3. **Working in this way creates a safe environment** where all ideas can see the light of day. Once the team begins working positively and constructively to improve an idea, the creator of the original idea feels valued and respected, and other team members who witness this can count on being treated with the same respect.

4. **Greenhouse Thinking™ strengthens teams.** Teams become stronger and more committed to the task when everyone feels valued and respected; they also become highly

productive as they work together quickly to reach their shared goals.

5: **Company commitment to the solutions gets stronger.** When using this technique the final action plans reflect implementation of "our idea" rather than "his idea" or "her idea" because the idea has grown, morphed and improved with everyone's input. This prevents the "not invented here" syndrome that kills so many great initiatives.

6. **Greenhouse Thinking™ is extremely efficient.** Once a list of ideas has been created many teams are tempted to discuss the drawbacks of each idea or group them into like categories. This wastes time working on dozens of ideas the team would never even consider. Greenhouse Thinking™ eliminates that trap by skimming the best ideas off the top and moving forward with those ideas ONLY. This step leaves lesser ideas, unnecessary grouping or other time wasters behind without a discussion or debate.

CHAPTER FOUR SUMMARY – THE CARE AND HANDLING OF FLEDGLING IDEAS

1. Approach all ideas with the question, "What do I like about this idea?"

2. Write down a list of specific things you like about the idea to use as starting points for new ideas.

3. As a second step, think about what's wrong with the idea and express a wish that *overcomes* each problem with a specific concrete solution.

4. Feel free to change the idea as needed, to remove undesirable factors, add positive qualities it does not yet have and mold the idea into something real, logical and practical.

5. As a final step, ask yourself "How can I make this a HUGE idea?" and push yourself to build it into something remarkable.

TIPS FOR PERSONAL PROBLEM SOLVING

1. If you are working alone on a personal problem, take any idea you have and make an extensive list of what you like, even if it seems obvious.

2. After listing likes, write down all your objections to the idea; then go back and systematically rephrase them into wishes.

3. Next, look at your likes and systematically turn each like into a new idea to solve your problem. Likes are often expressions of benefits you are seeking.

4. Finally, push yourself to express concrete solutions with each wish instead of restating a negative. For example, if you are trying to lose weight and wish to not be hungry, try wishing for the positive—I wish to feel full and satisfied—because that suggests solutions more directly than stating a negative.

TIPS FOR BUSINESS PROBLEM SOLVING

1. Insist that your team discusses ALL the likes before bringing up any negatives or wishes. Keep pushing for more by saying, "What else do you like?" "What else?"

2. Use a flip chart or white board to accurately write down each "like" stated by a team member. To ensure participants feel heard, do not change the idea or language in any way. Any rephrasing you do to another person's idea tells them the original idea wasn't good enough, and that it needed to be changed.

3. Open up the discussion to wishes only after all the likes have been listed. As your team expresses wishes and you write them down, listen for negative language like "I wish product spoilage wouldn't happen," and challenge the participant to rephrase it into something they DO want such as "I wish to ensure the product always stays very fresh." Making something positive happen is much easier than preventing a negative.

CHAPTER FIVE

IDENTIFYING AND BREAKING YOUR ASSUMPTIONS

This chapter explores ways to free yourself from unneeded constraints, so you can create breakthrough solutions that really work.

While the CPS process is simple—diverge without judgment, then converge on top ideas—breaking our preconceived notions of "truth" is much more difficult. It goes back to those same Kindergarten lessons I mentioned earlier, when the teacher told us that it's "wrong" to color a cow purple but "right" to color it brown. In this same way we learn absolute "truths" about the world around us that box our thinking in without us even being aware it's happening.

These truths emerge as assumptions, and we all have dozens of them in the back of our minds which greatly affect how we approach a problem.

WHAT ARE "ASSUMPTIONS?"

According to CPS, assumptions are the constraints we put on ourselves when trying to solve a problem, sometimes without even being aware we are limiting ourselves. We all play with two kinds of assumptions: those we know about and can identify, and those we aren't aware we have. Known assumptions can be addressed; unknown cannot unless you dig deep to find them.

EXAMPLES OF KNOWN ASSUMPTIONS

A classic riddle illustrates assumption-busting perfectly. Have you seen the "Nine Dot" puzzle? The challenge is to connect all nine dots using four continuous straight lines.

It isn't until you break out of the invisible "box" made by the nine dots that you can find the answer.

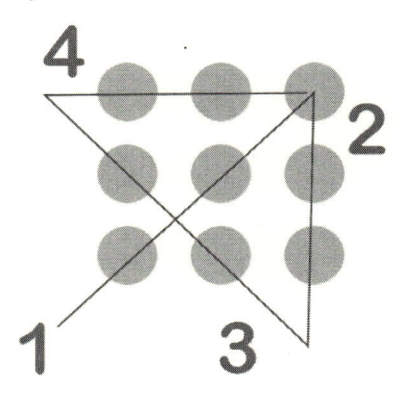

47

Let's try the exercise again, this time using only one straight line instead of four.

How might you do it? As you ponder that, think about what assumptions you're making and list them.

1. Assume we're using a small tip pen/pencil/marker → what if we had a wide brush?

2. Assume the paper must stay whole → what if we cut or tore the paper to line up three rows on top of each other?

3. Assume the paper must stay flat and unfolded → what if we folded the paper so each dot is on top of the other

4. Assume dots and paper don't move → what if we put the paper on a moving turntable and drew a line from center to edge as dots are turning?

These examples represent known assumptions. While you may not be aware of them at first, they come to mind once you decide to list them systematically. The benefits of identifying and breaking your known assumptions are significant:

- You become aware of the limiting thoughts you may not know you have.

48

- You have the opportunity to question each assumption and rid yourself of those that you know are not real.

- Your thinking changes from negative (barriers) to positive (possibilities).

- You wind up with truly breakthrough solutions, e.g. tear the paper to connect the dots!

PROCESS TO USE FOR BREAKING ASSUMPTIONS

To free yourself from constraints:

1. List ALL of your assumptions about the problem.

Imagine you want a new home but believe you can't afford it. Your assumptions might include:

- I can't get a loan.
- I'll never find something I love that's affordable.
- Moving is expensive.
- I can't afford my desired location.

2. Now BREAK your assumptions by finding 1-5 ideas that counter each one.

Using the example above:

- I can't get a loan →
    - Apply for credit union loans.
    - Look into HUD for section 8 housing.
    - Consider crowd funding.
    - Rent to own.

- o   Find a gift registry for housing funds.

- I'll never find something I love that's affordable →
  - o   Buy a fixer-upper to make my own.
  - o   Buy a half-constructed house to finish to my taste.
  - o   Save longer, rent and wait for the perfect place to come to market.
  - o   Buy land outside of town and build the house myself.

- Moving is expensive →
  - o   Recruit college students in exchange for beer and pizza.
  - o   Host a moving party and invite your friends.
  - o   Move slowly over several weeks, one carload a day.

- I can't afford my desired location →
  - o   Try condos instead of houses in your location.
  - o   Take your time and wait for the perfect opportunity.
  - o   Check with neighborhood homeowners regularly, to nab a home before it gets to market, so you save on realtor commission.
  - O   Look for a fixer-upper to buy affordably now and fix it up over time.
  - O   Consider splitting a home purchase with one or more roommates.

EXAMPLES OF UNKNOWN ASSUMPTIONS

Now let's take a real business example—one currently being addressed. A premium chocolates manufacturer does 90% of its business between November 1 and December 31 which is far less than ideal. Revenue comes from a combination of online sales and sales in the company's 500 chocolate shops around the country.

Because of the need to stay as fresh as possible, company leaders support just-in-time production to ensure their products have the highest quality taste and appearance. That means 100% of production takes place between August 1 and October 31 every year. Now add the fact that the company has three production plants across the U.S. and 500 chocolate shops with backroom production facilities that remain idle most of the year.

The inefficiency is staggering.

In its search for a more streamlined solution, the company is considering a complete reorganization of both production and distribution, to eliminate inefficiencies. The obvious first solution is to close two plants and all back-of-shop production, and produce everything from the one remaining plant location.

In this case, some of the company's obvious assumptions include, "We want to remain a seasonal business instead of finding products to sell in our off season" and "We want our business to continue to be 90% holiday, and that will not change."

But even more important--and more difficult to identify—are the assumptions we DON'T KNOW we are making. These assumptions become so ingrained in our consciousness that we don't even think to question them. For our chocolates manufacturer some unknown assumptions, or as I like to call them, "duh!" assumptions include:

- Production takes place at a centralized factory.
- Factories are built of brick and mortar and are permanent installations.
- Our proprietary production process is our competitive advantage, which cannot be shared or outsourced due to security concerns.

Now let's systematically break the rules and "bust" each assumption.

- Production is centralized →
    - Decentralize production to minimize shipping costs and improve product freshness and quality.
    - Close both factories and use retail back rooms of chocolate shops around the country as localized mini-factories.

- Factories are brick and mortar, permanent locations →

    - We have temporary pop-up stores, why not pop-up factories?
    - Use an efficiency algorithm to schedule production in different locations, depending on where business is sourced. This approach ensures that production always happens when and where it's needed, keeps inventory low and saves shipping costs.
    - Create portable, temperature-controlled semi-truck or shipping-container "factories" for just-in-time production; roll it in for the season and store the container when not in use.

- Our proprietary production process is a secret →
    - Consider partnering with a professional co-packer you can trust, using an airtight legal agreement that keeps the competitive advantage a secret.
    - Invite only employees to work in the temporary factories, to keep the secret in house.

In the end, by "busting" our business assumptions—especially the ingrained assumptions we would never have thought of— we found an extremely innovative solution: pop-up factories in shipping containers built to the company's specifications. Containers are locked and stored when not in use. During the high season, only employees are allowed to drive containers up to the distribution center, lock them onto the docking bay and produce from inside the containers. When the season is over employees un-dock the containers, lock them up and store them away.

Knowing how to bust assumptions gives you the power to break through even the toughest problems.

CHAPTER FIVE SUMMARY – BREAKING THROUGH ASSUMPTIONS TO AVOID UNNECESSARY CONSTRAINTS

1. List all the assumptions you are making.

2. Then push yourself further to write down the "duh!" assumptions—the ones you aren't even aware you're making.

3. *Systematically break through* each one with a few possible solutions that do not support the assumption.

TIPS FOR PERSONAL PROBLEM SOLVING

1. This exercise is difficult to do without editing yourself. Start by writing down your assumptions and push it as far as you can without letting yourself reject an idea before you get it down on paper.

2. If you get stuck, push yourself on the "duh!" ideas—those that are so obvious you wouldn't bother to mention them.

3. Ignore feasibility for now—break the rules by asking, "What if X?" Or, "What if this assumption were not true?"

TIPS FOR BUSINESS PROBLEM SOLVING

1. Watch out for sacred cows! These assumptions are so hard-wired into the collective consciousness of a company that simply mentioning them can be risky. When that happens, remind yourself that any idea good enough to significantly challenge a sacred cow is likely to be so new and valuable

that you may be forgiven for questioning the unquestionable. I would also argue that managers have a duty to question sacred cows, in order to move with the times and stay relevant.

2. If you can't break through either identifying the assumptions or coming up with innovative ideas to break them wide open, consult a company newbie—someone whose tenure is shorter than yours. The longer you work within a corporate culture the greater your internal knowledge and alignment, and therefore the larger your blinders become. You, too, have "drunk the Kool-Aid" of groupthink that naturally occurs within any like-minded collection of people. This is especially true for those who use and value facts, because the more you know the less you assume. For those reasons, a newer employee will naturally have a fresher perspective.

3. Consultants or other outsiders with whom you've partnered and built trust can also be extremely helpful in identifying assumptions and constraints that you may not see at first glance because of your depth of knowledge.

SECTION II:
THE CPS PROCESS

CHAPTER SIX

FINDING THE RIGHT PROBLEM STATEMENT

This chapter focuses on how to determine which problem you want to work on, and why it's so important to choose the right problem.

WHAT IS THE RIGHT PROBLEM?

The right problem is the problem statement that most closely represents your true challenge, without limiting your options.

Why is it so important to identify the *right* problem? This well-known urban legend illustrates the dangers of working with the first problem statement that comes to mind:

> In the 1970s, as land became more expensive, many hotel companies began building hotel "towers." As soon as a property would open, guests complained frequently about the slow elevators. In response, one company hired a team of Swiss engineers that specialize in elevator technology. After tinkering with the elevator for over a year, they succeeded in speeding up the elevators by one second per floor.

Unfortunately, after all that time and money was spent, guest complaints continued unabated . . . until one employee suggested hanging mirrors at every elevator bank, to distract guests from the wait. With this action—a far cheaper alternative to high-speed elevator technology—guest complaints completely disappeared.

In the example above, the problem statement "How to eliminate guest complaints about elevator wait time" would have been much more appropriate than the problem statement they used: "How to shorten elevator wait time." Working on the right problem yielded more affordable and effective solutions.

As Steven Covey says in his wildly successful book, *The Seven Habits of Highly Effective People (1989)*, "If the ladder is not leaning against the right wall, every step we take just gets us to the wrong place."

Moral: Address the RIGHT problem.

PROCESS FOR DEFINING PROBLEMS

The process of identifying the right problem statement is simple:

1. Define your problem.

To define a problem, begin the statement with the words, "How to . . ." For example, a problem statement about personal income might be, "How to have plenty of income without working." A problem about business growth could be stated, "How to grow business 10% this fiscal year." This sounds easy because we all know what our problems are. However, it's also easy to make a mistake by jumping in to solve the first problem that comes to mind. The first problem may not be the right problem, which can lead to wrong solutions.

To ensure you "lean your ladder on the right wall" and focus on the right problem, take some time to generate at least a dozen "how to" statements that represent multiple perspectives on your problem. Often this can be accomplished by paraphrasing the original problem.

The personal problem above could be stated in several ways:

- How to have plenty of money without working
- How to retire now comfortably
- How to feel abundance without income
- How to build wealth using current resources
- How to amass more money than I'm worth
- How to finance my life without income

As you can see, multiple aspects begin to emerge as you state your problem in different ways, which allows you to select the problem statement that will make the biggest impact on your issue.

2. Set criteria to decide on the problem statement that will make the greatest impact.

Once you've identified a range of problem statements, end the divergence portion of the process and begin to converge on the highest potential statement. First, set criteria for selection by answering the question, "What needs to be true of a problem statement for me to want to work on it?"

If you're solving a personal problem, high-level criteria to select your best problem statement might include:

    1. Fits my values

    2. Has high potential to address my issue

3. Is comprehensive enough to be effective

To solve a business problem consider high-level criteria such as:

1. Focuses on a business or customer need

2. Fits the company's/brand's values and equities

3. Has the potential to make a large business impact

At this point do NOT consider cost or feasibility for either personal or business criteria—it's too soon and can make brainstorming nearly impossible. If you self-edit most of your ideas you will inadvertently close off some great options—like the highly feasible and profitable mirror solution to the hotel's elevator problem. Once you identify the right problem, you'll have plenty of opportunity to apply those constraints.

For example, one paraphrase from the personal problem above that might be considered not feasible is, "How to have plenty of money without working" because it seems unrealistic. But if you were to reject this option outright you would miss the opportunity to think about passive income streams, investment options, backing someone else's business, etc.—all of which would be great ways to accomplish a goal that seems infeasible at first blush.

3. Select the problem statements that best meet the criteria.

Don't measure each problem statement against each criterion; instead, use criteria together to create a mindset that will aid your gut in determining either "Yes, this is a big problem" (vote for it!) or "No, this is not a big problem" (pass it up). You're looking for a simple "yes" or "no."

If you're working with a team, have everyone vote for at least one third of the problem statements, to ensure overlap. Then re-order all the statements from the top number of votes received down to 0 votes.

DO NOT GROUP STATEMENTS BEFORE VOTING—that will eliminate uniqueness in ideas and reduce your options considerably.

This simple process WILL give you the right problem statement to ensure you find the best possible solutions.

CHAPTER SIX SUMMARY – ADDRESSING THE RIGHT PROBLEM

1. It's extremely important to select the *right* problem.

2. To find it, generate a large quantity of problem statements that represent multiple perspectives on the issue.

3. Set broad criteria to evaluate all the problem statements.

4. Select the best statement: one that's broad enough to be inclusive and cast a wide net, but also defined enough to ensure strategic focus and action.

TIPS FOR PERSONAL PROBLEM SOLVING

1. Challenge yourself to take multiple perspectives as you look for the right problem statement.

2. Push yourself to come up with at least 20 statements, remembering not to censor your thinking.

3. Setting criteria is easier if you think about the specific qualities a great problem statement will have. Use that as guidance to build your list of evaluation criteria.

4. Select one—and only one—statement.

TIPS FOR BUSINESS PROBLEM SOLVING

1. Look at your starting problem as "How to [accomplish something positive.]"

2. Avoid the temptation to accept the first problem statement suggested. Instead, look for alternative statements and suggest others to ensure you land on the right problem. You'll save your company a significant amount of time and money by identifying the right problem the first time around.

3. As you set criteria, remember you are ultimately looking for a problem statement that balances the right amount of breadth/inclusiveness with the right amount of specificity and focus.

4. As you select your final problem statement, be sure your broader team is aligned with it, to ensure the upcoming group brainstorming work gets off to an enthusiastic start.

CHAPTER SEVEN

THE ART AND POWER OF WISHING

Brand new ideas often start with a simple wish—something we learned to do as children when we approached a fountain, glimpsed the first star in the night sky or stared down the glaring candles on a birthday cake. Unfortunately as we've become more mired in real-world practicality, many of us have forgotten how to wish.

Rekindling your ability to wish can provide a powerful tool for breaking through truly tough problems.

In CPS, wishing takes place as a first step. When I conduct a brainstorm session, I introduce the topic and give participants about 45 minutes for open wishing. Then we review the themes to identify strategic territory that emerged and choose three or four as areas of strategic focus.

WHAT IS A CPS WISH?

Simply start with the words "I wish" and complete the sentence by expressing an unmet need or desire. Keep in mind that this is not intended to be a concrete solution with the words "I wish" put in front of it.

For example, if we were looking for something fun to do this weekend we might say, "I wish to experience something new this weekend," which suggests many different options. A more specific solution disguised as a wish, like, "I wish to have dinner at the popular restaurant, Butcher & Boar this Saturday night" would be less helpful because it doesn't take us into any new territory. We're looking for broad wishes that offer many possible solutions.

Let's consider this example problem, "How to increase our current business over the next six months." Helpful, broad wishes might include:

- I wish our company were universally known throughout the world.
- I wish for free publicity on our emerging technologies, to showcase their benefits to the greater community, beyond just the benefits to our company.
- I wish all prospective customers understood our key points of difference.

Note that every statement allows for a long list of possible concrete solutions. In this case, there are many, many ways to increase global awareness of a company, including advertising, creating global business alliances, participating in state trade missions overseas, networking at global conferences, creating a PR campaign and so much more.

To determine whether your wish is a helpful one apply a quick test by asking yourself, "Can I find many solutions within this wish?" If the answer is "yes," you are wishing at the right level of detail.

WHY WISH?

The benefit of starting CPS with broad wishes is to map out strategic territory quickly and efficiently. From the wishes above several themes or territories have already emerged:

- Building broad awareness among prospects
- Pursuing a global reputation
- Utilizing low cost communication options
- Publicizing via collaboration with civic leaders
- Communicating key points of difference
- Identifying the right prospects

Three simple "I wish" statements produced at least six possible territories from which dozens of concrete solutions can emerge.

WHAT ARE THE TYPES OF WISHES?

Below are six types of wishes. Strive to use each type at least once and you will be guaranteed a large map of fruitful strategic territories.

1. **Paraphrase the problem statement in your own words.**
    If the problem is "How to increase our current business" a useful paraphrase might be "I wish to grow the business we have." While similar to the original statement, this one takes a slightly different point of view, focusing on growth via current capabilities.

2. **Interpret a certain aspect of the problem.**
    A wish that focuses on one part of the above problem could be, "I wish to sell our current products to new

customers." This wish offers something new—the idea of focusing on current products for new customers versus new products for current customers.

3. **Use constructive misunderstanding.**

    This is a fun one! Sometimes when we misunderstand another teammate's idea or wish, the misunderstanding can actually provide a useful way to come at the problem from a different angle. For example, if the statement, "I wish to sell our products to new customers" were to be misunderstood as "I wish to sell our products to *few* customers" (in other words, focus our efforts) we would suddenly have a new perspective around consolidating business to the most profitable markets.

4. **Add a fresh perspective with Opposition Wishing.**

    During a brainstorm session you may disagree with a direction—this is common. Instead of being disruptive or negative you can use an Opposition Wish to surface the objection constructively. For example, if you don't like the statement, "I wish for few customers so we can focus our efforts," use the opportunity to offer another perspective: "I wish for MORE customers, to spread out our risk." Now you have two opposite perspectives, both of which are valid and helpful. And it surfaced without discussion or argument.

5. **Widen the lens with Associations Wishes.**

    As wishing continues, it's useful to expand into new areas. One fast, easy way is to use an Associations Wish—anything outside the problem that you associate with the problem. For example, for the statement, "I wish to sell our products to few customers," an Association Wish might be, "I wish for military customers as our new business target." In this case the participant associated "the few, the proud" (the Marines' slogan) with the "few" customers statement to create an entirely new perspective.

6. **Imagine perfection with Utopian Wishes.**

   This is my favorite because it quickly identifies the perfect-world scenario so we can work *toward* it. When using this, you must completely ignore the laws of the land, the laws of physics and your moral compass—no constraints whatsoever are allowed. For example, consider this utopian wish "I wish to wake up tomorrow morning to find our business magically grown to twice the size." Of course this would never happen on its own, but using this type of wish opens up the new territory of quickly *doubling* the size of the business, allowing the team to search for other ways to achieve it that *are* practical, that *do* follow the laws of the land and the laws of physics.

The next time you hear a child—or an adult for that matter—make a wish, take a moment to think about the unmet need underneath it. What you learn can be amusing as well as revealing.

CHAPTER SEVEN SUMMARY – THE ART AND POWER OF WISHING

1. A wish in CPS is simply a statement beginning with "I wish" that expresses a broad need or desire, not a specific solution.

2. Wishing in CPS is a fast and powerful way to get dozens of unmet needs on the table very quickly.

3. There are several types of wishes, each type taking you to new opportunities. Try them all out and find your favorites.

4. A wish is always positive—it's something you want, rather than something you don't want.

TIPS FOR PERSONAL PROBLEM SOLVING

1. When working alone it can be tempting to start out being very practical. Stretch yourself by liberally using the higher level wishes, including Opposition Wishing, Associations Wishing and Utopian Wishing.

2. Get into the practice of thinking, "What do I wish for?" This will keep you in a positive mindset and enable you to better and more quickly begin to understand yourself and your personal needs.

TIPS FOR BUSINESS PROBLEM SOLVING

1. Take a moment to teach your group how to wish broadly. Explain that each wish represents a broad unmet need or desired value. Many specific solutions will fit within each wish.

2. If you hear a specific idea expressed in wish form—"I wish for a spreadsheet that adjusts forecasts with actual daily shipments and recalculates," for example—ask your participant to articulate the need behind the wish. Get the contributor to elaborate or generalize that specific solution to something at a higher level, like, "I wish our forecasting became more and more accurate with each day." A wish at this level is much easier to work with and address.

3. Push your team to try out the high-level wishes, including Opposition, Association and Utopian. These types of wishes produce the most forward-thinking ideas.

4. Do not allow participants to build on wishes. Building, by its very nature, creates more specificity which is not helpful at this juncture because we are looking for broad themes.

CHAPTER EIGHT

SELECTING STRATEGIC TERRITORY FOR BRAINSTORMING

As we discussed in the last chapter, divergence often begins by wishing broadly without any constraints, which allows the team to express their unmet needs or desires. After 30-45 minutes, it's time to stop wishing and start digging into wishes in order to extract "territory" as strategic focus.

WHAT IS A TERRITORY?

A territory is a broad theme that suggests a long list of possible concrete solutions. Like the wish it came from, the territory often represents an unmet need or unfulfilled desire.

For example, let's assume your problem is "How to have fun this weekend." You might wish for many things you desire or need:

- I wish to experience something new and exciting.
- I wish to take advantage of the great weather.
- I wish to get physical exercise while having fun.

As you listen for underlying themes several territories emerge as options:

- Exploring
- Going somewhere new
- Adding excitement to my weekend
- New activities I've yet to experience
- Learning a new skill
- Nature activities
- Physical activities
- Social activities outdoors
- Exercise with friends

WHY DO WE NEED TERRITORIES?

Identifying territories provides strategic focus for your brainstorming to ensure you address and continue to stay focused on the right problem. Brainstorming naturally creates "drift" in the conversation, as one idea leads to another thought and then to another idea; however, without structure the discussion can easily continue until the original purpose is totally forgotten.

A few years ago I participated in a financial services project focusing on new product ideas for a large credit card client. They used an online brainstorming tool from a tech supplier that allows everyone to contribute ideas at once but does not allow for the creation of territory. Brainstorming of new credit card ideas quickly and easily drifted into a discussion of the aches and pains of pregnancy. Really. One contributor suggested an idea for a credit card perfect for pregnant women, and off it went into dozens of irrelevant comments about the world of pregnancy, never to return to financial services! This kind of drifting is a constant challenge and not at all helpful to problem solving.

HOW DO WE FIND TERRITORY?

All you have to do is listen to broad wishes and jot down common themes that emerge during wishing. Be sure these are big territories that represent a large number of opportunities. A territory that might be considered too small within this particular example would be "hiking outdoors." A better territory might be "nature activities" because it represents so many more options.

HOW DO WE PRIORITIZE TERRITORIES?

First, list all the broad themes that come to mind from your wishing session. Then, decide on criteria you'd like to use to prioritize the themes. Typical criteria include:

- Territory is rich with opportunity for solutions.
- Territory has high potential to solve the problem.
- Territory is important enough to warrant spending the time and energy required to address it.

Then, with your criteria in mind you can prioritize in one of two ways.

1. VOTE – If you are working with a group of up to 20 participants:

    - Count the number of possible territories listed and divide by three, to determine the number of votes each team member gets. (X number of votes = number of territories/3)

- Put a letter in front of each territory, starting with item "A."
- Ask participants to select X number of territories they personally feel are fruitful and write those letters on their page.
- Count votes for each lettered territory by asking for a show of hands.
- Start the discussion on the top priority.

2. RATE – If you are working alone:

- Look at each theme or territory with your criteria in mind.
- Rate each theme according to its ability to meet the criteria, using a scale of 0-5, with 0 meaning "no interest" in pursuing that territory and 5 meaning "extremely interested."
    - Look at each rating to determine what rose to the top.
    - Begin by addressing that territory.

As you may have noticed, I did not provide options for working with a group of over 20—that's because brainstorming with more than 20 people creates sophisticated challenges that should not be attempted by an unskilled practitioner. So don't do it!

CHAPTER EIGHT SUMMARY – SELECTING STRATEGIC TERRITORY FOR BRAINSTORMING

1. Review all your wishes and list all the themes they represent.

2. Set criteria to help you select the best territories.

3. If you're working with a team, allow them to vote for the best ideas on the list. To determine the number of votes each person gets, divide the number of wishes by three. (For example, if you have listed thirty wishes, each member of your team should get ten votes.)

4. If you're working alone, rate each wish on how likely it is to solve the problem, using a scale from 0-5; you can give all 0s, all 5s or anything in between. Then use your ratings to identify the top two or three territories you want to address.

TIPS FOR PERSONAL PROBLEM SOLVING

1. Your gut may tell you which topics will be most fruitful; if that happens, go with your gut.

2. If you feel stuck, use the rating system described above.

3. Consider asking others to help you select the right territory, just to get an outside perspective. Use their input as "advisory" only and make your own best decision.

TIPS FOR BUSINESS PROBLEM SOLVING

1. If at all possible, let your team weigh in on the territories by voting or rating, instead of allowing one or two higher-level

managers to make the decision without input. The more inclusive your session, the greater your team's energy and commitment will be to a quality outcome.

2. Once the key decision-maker is ready to choose final territories of focus, offer your team's selections as guidance instead of insisting the votes alone determine the team's decisions. While inclusiveness builds trust, results pay the bills. As you did with the problem statement, you'll need to choose the right territories to reach your end goal successfully.

3. To avoid wasting a lot of time, begin by choosing the first two territories only. Because territories naturally overlap, you'll discover that in the process of choosing the first two, you may have already covered topic number three in great detail and are ready to move on to a different territory.

CHAPTER NINE

EXCURSION THEORY: CREATING BRILLIANT IDEAS ON DEMAND

Now that you know about wishing and identifying strategic territory, we can begin to brainstorm dozens of possible ideas or solutions. It sounds easy, but here's the tough part: creating all those brilliant solutions on the spot, under pressure, to ensure we have lots of great ideas to choose from.

Let's talk about where ideas come from. We all get ideas—they can come from absolutely anywhere as the result of a simple electrical connection within your brain.

Your brain is an amazing tool for any number of reasons, but especially as it relates to brainstorming. It's like a HUGE database with billions of files and documents that contain information about your entire life experience—your genetic and family background, your formal education, that inspirational kindergarten teacher, your second grade best friend, your first kiss, that funny thing Aunt Mary said at Christmas 2011, your relationship with your first boss—literally everything that makes you, well... YOU. And everything in that database is fair game for finding brand new ideas. All it takes is a simple connection between one of your many unique life experiences and the problem at hand.

Often, ideas just "come" to us. Think about it: Where are you when you get your best ideas? When I ask participants that question, they say things like, "In the shower . . . when I'm first waking up . . . while driving . . . when I'm dropping off to sleep . . . while hiking . . . doing a mundane task." While the activities may be different, they all represent "down time" for the brain— when great ideas just come to you, your brain is at rest. CPS calls this *incubation*.

I don't know about you, but in my world no one has the luxury of waiting around for an idea to strike. Fortunately, we *can* use carefully crafted mental "excursions" to find new ideas when we build in incubation time.

WHAT IS AN EXCURSION?

Just like it sounds, an excursion is a small mental "trip" to another environment or experience, in order to borrow ideas and bring them to your problem. An excursion can take many different forms, which include the use of role-playing, metaphors related to the problem, word association, physical field trips and much more. You can even use a daydream to create new ideas.

WHY DO WE NEED EXCURSIONS?

Let's talk for a moment about the power of different types of thinking. In the chart below, the bottom axis shows the degree of novelty or "newness" within an idea, beginning with old, been-there-done-that ideas, and pushing the scale out to totally new-to-the-world ideas. The vertical axis represents different types of thinking, starting with logical, rational thinking, moving up toward analogous thinking, and reaching all the way up to fantasy or futuristic thinking. We live in the business world, so we don't push it beyond that, but theoretically one could go even further with the assistance of peyote, hypnotism, or other means . . . we'll stay safely below that mark!

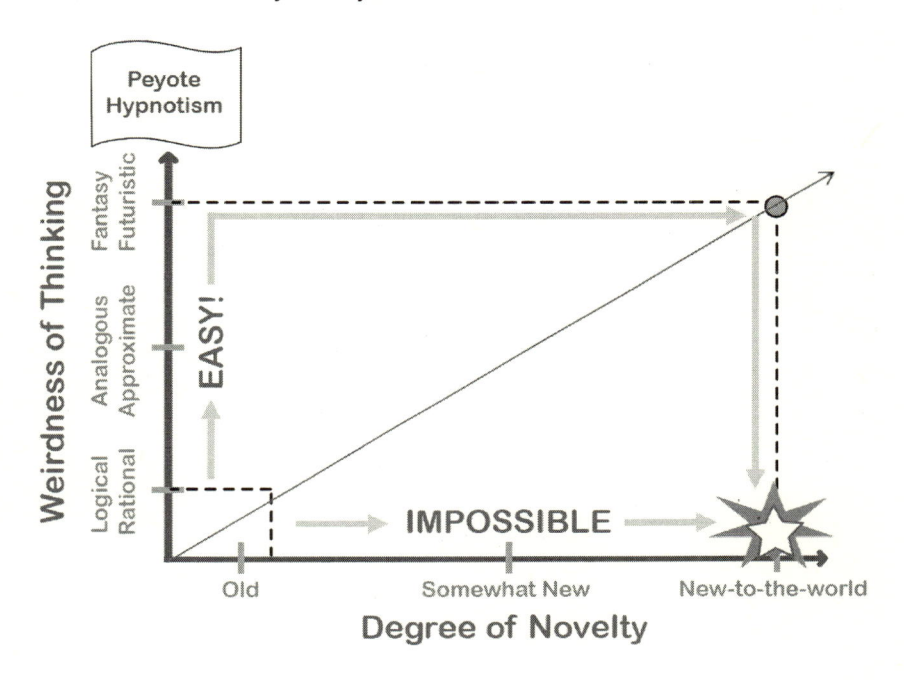

[Figure: A graph with "Weirdness of Thinking" on the vertical axis (Logical/Rational, Analogous/Approximate, Fantasy/Futuristic, with a flag above marked "Peyote Hypnotism") and "Degree of Novelty" on the horizontal axis (Old, Somewhat New, New-to-the-world). A diagonal line shows "EASY!" path. A horizontal arrow labeled "IMPOSSIBLE" points from Old to New-to-the-world at the Logical/Rational level, ending in a starburst. A gray dot sits at the upper right corner.]

At the end of the day, you need to walk away with logical, rational, new-to-the-world ideas. Ironically, that won't happen by sticking to logical and rational thinking. From years of experience I can tell you that it is impossible to make an old, logical and practical idea new.

Not until you push yourself up into analogous or fantasy thinking will you easily come up with something truly novel. Let's face it--it's not enough to have new-to-the-world ideas if they are pure fantasy (as indicated by the gray dot in the upper right corner of the chart.) If it's a la-la-land idea, who cares if it's new? It will never see the light of day in its current form.

In contrast to the impossibility of making old ideas new, it's very easy to make a brand new fantasy idea real. Apply Greenhouse Thinking™ to it so you can drive it down to logical/rational *and* new to the world. That is the gold standard of brainstorming: completely novel ideas that are logical and actually work in the real world.

HOW DO EXCURSIONS WORK?

Fortunately, you can use mental excursions to climb up the "weirdness of thinking" scale by following a very fast, six-step process:

1. Announce the topic of the brainstorm (grounding).

2. For just a moment, forget the topic of the brainstorm (don't worry, it's safely tucked away in the back of your mind).

3. Go "somewhere else" mentally (the excursion).

4. Incubate (quiet brain processing time).

5. Force Fit (topic + excursion = new idea).

6. Write down your new idea and share it ("brilliance on demand!")

NOW PLAY IT OUT

Let's take it more slowly by examining a real-world example. Imagine we are working for a home exercise equipment manufacturer who wants to generate new product ideas that are fun and provide exercise for kids who are 8-10 years old. To announce the six-step process you might use a script like this:

1. "In just a moment we will be generating ideas for new products that make exercise fun for kids age 8-10" (announce the topic of the brainstorm as grounding).

2. "Now forget that topic for just a moment" (forget the topic of the brainstorm, as it's safely tucked away in the back of your mind).

3. "Instead, think about kids in the broadest sense, and write down five activities that are fun for them (go somewhere else mentally—the excursion.) For example, kids love...imagination games." [Pause and allow the team to complete this task.]

4. "Now, be quiet for a moment" (incubate, quiet brain processing time)....

5. "...as you force fit your idea to the problem" (fun kids' exercise + imagination games = new idea). [Pause again to be sure the room is silent for this activity.]

6. "Finally, write down your new idea." This group's brilliance-on-demand idea was a kid-sized treadmill programmed to create physical gaming fantasies with all activity 100% self-powered. Kids use the hand and leg sensors to make their "avatar" run uphill and downhill over terrain, bend down to

gather tools, throw and catch objects, mix potions, complete challenges, etc.

HOW DO I CHOOSE THE BEST EXCURSION FOR THE TOPIC?

The objective of any excursion is to make the creative task of idea generation as easy as possible for participants. To determine which excursion to use, first think about the key ATTRIBUTE of your problem and tie your excursion to that idea. For example, if your problem is "How to make exercise fun for kids," take the concept of "fun for kids" and look at other items or activities that share the attribute. What's fun for kids? We know they like mystery, extreme flavors, discovery, hanging out with friends, playing video games, etc. Once you have a list, apply the ideas to the topic at hand.

Similarly, if your problem is "How to increase efficiency in my business," apply the concept of efficiency from other arenas and ask how a company like UPS for example—or another company you think of as being highly effective—creates efficiency. Make a list. Then look at the list to see whether any of their efficiencies can be applied to your business. You can even take it farther by asking, "How does LEAN manufacturing look at efficiency?" Or even, "What does a single mother below the poverty line do to make her spending more efficient?"

ANYTHING--AND I MEAN ANYTHING—CAN BE AN EXCURSION

Now let's see how far we can take our excursion theory, while testing the assertion that anything at all can be an excursion.

We'll start with a fun activity to include in a brainstorming session: After you've been together for an hour, ask each member of the team to divulge one thing they daydreamed about at some time during the previous hour. People daydream regardless of how interesting the meeting, and here's why: The average meeting takes place at 150 words per minute but the average brain processes information at 800 words per minute. That means each person has, at any given time, 650 words per minute of unused brain capacity that *must* go somewhere. That's where daydreams come in.

Consider some of the daydreams participants have described over the years when I've asked, "What did you think about this morning that had nothing to do with our meeting?" People have said:

- "I wonder if my daughter remembered her lunch before getting on the school bus."
- "I'm thinking about the concert we're seeing on Friday."
- "My mind went to the meeting at the office that I'm missing this morning."
- "I thought about when I can make it to the farmer's market this weekend."
- "I need to do laundry this weekend."
- And many other mundane, real-world thoughts

We can apply these daydreams to the problem mentioned above about kids' exercise by following these steps:

1. Announce the topic: new products that make exercise fun for kids 8-10.

2. Forget the topic.

3. Think about your daydream—the concert we're seeing Friday.

4. Provide quiet time for incubation.

5. Force fit: Friday concert + fun kids' exercise = ?

6. Write down the new idea: a video game synced to small musical light boxes placed around the room. Players must wait for the music and then race to reach each box before its light goes out and the tune is over; then another box lights up. If you hit each light box in time, an entire song is played.

To summarize, getting ideas any time you need them is a very simple proposition. Just "go somewhere else" mentally, borrow an idea, and bring it back to the problem.

CHAPTER NINE SUMMARY – CREATING BRILLIANT IDEAS ON DEMAND

1. Take a little mental "excursion" or "trip" to another arena and borrow an idea to apply to your problem.

2. Follow the six-step process whether working alone or in a group:
   a. Announce the topic.
   b. Forget the topic.
   c. Go "somewhere else" and find an idea.
   d. Incubate.
   e. Force fit the idea to your problem.
   f. Write down your new idea.

3. Remember that literally anything can be used as an excursion, from a recent daydream you had, to looking out the window, to finding a random object, and much more.

TIPS FOR PERSONAL PROBLEM SOLVING

1. If you are doing this alone, solidify your learning by following the steps slowly and carefully as you begin to use the six-step process.

2. As you are choosing your own excursion, look for one that has a concept in common with your problem, to make it as easy as possible to create new ideas.

3. If you find yourself getting stuck, use some of the excursion options listed in the next chapter.

TIPS FOR BUSINESS PROBLEM SOLVING

1. If you're leading a group, plan your excursions carefully, to make sure they will work. Play them out—if the excursions are difficult for you, they will be even more difficult for your participants. Make them fun and easy.

2. As you lead your group, give ONLY ONE instruction, one step at a time. Wait for the team to finish that task, and then give the next instruction. If you give three instructions at once, two will be forgotten.

3. Choose excursions that have a concept in common with your problem, to make it as easy as possible for your team to create new ideas.

4. If you find yourself getting stuck, try some of the excursion options listed in the next chapter.

CHAPTER TEN

EXCURSION TOOLS AND TECHNIQUES

Many people find brainstorming to be fun! That's because the tools and techniques required to create new ideas get us thinking in new and different ways. Excursions are "brain games" of sorts. Just think about your problem, play a little brain game (go somewhere else to borrow an idea), and tie the two thoughts together.

In Chapter Nine, we reviewed the six steps used for any excursion:

1. Announce the topic.
2. Forget the topic.
3. Excursion: mentally go "somewhere else" to borrow an idea.
4. Incubate.
5. Force fit topic + idea = new idea.
6. Write down your new idea.

In this chapter, we will focus on STEP THREE and show you all the different "places" we can go in our minds to find new ideas. We will introduce several different excursion activities, starting

89

with the logical/practical thinking all the way up to fantasy thinking. And we will track these excursions on the chart below from Chapter Nine, to help you understand where each option fits on the vertical axis; this will help you select the best excursion to use in the moment, factoring in:

- **The topic:** What are we working on? On which key attributes should we put our focus?

- **The thinking styles of your participants**: What are the thinking styles in the room and what types of exercises would be easy for this team? If they're linear, list-building is easy. If participants are more lateral, role-playing or metaphor work would be easier.

- **The energy level in the room**: What's the time of day? Is it first thing in the morning and the team doesn't know each other well yet? Choose solo activities early, and team people up for collaboration after the team is warmed up.

    Is it right after lunch and your team feels like having a quick snooze? Ask people to pair up and work together standing at a flip chart and present back to the group. This will be far more energizing than asking them to reflect quietly on an issue as they digest their food. Someone *always* nods off to sleep when I make this mistake.

- **How "breakthrough" our solution needs to be**: Think about the level of difficulty associated with the problem, and also how important truly novel, futuristic solutions are to success. Does the issue center on improving your product? If so, we need a close-in exercise that zeroes in on all the different product attributes, to make each one just a little bit better. On the other hand, if we're looking for a brand new way to feed babies that doesn't involve a breast or a bottle (yes, I did a project on this!) the topic requires more stretch thinking and therefore calls for more fantasy or futuristic exercises.

LOGICAL, PRACTICAL EXCURSIONS

These excursions are easy and work particularly well with a group of linear thinkers. As we saw in Chapter Three, linear thinkers prefer to work within the context of the problem to find their solutions. The three excursions described below, plus their variations, work well as a place to start with a corporate team. You can begin your session with the easy stuff and work your way up to more difficult exercises.

1. Attribute List-building: This is the easiest excursion of all, which is why it's listed at the bottom of the vertical axis on our Excursion Chart:

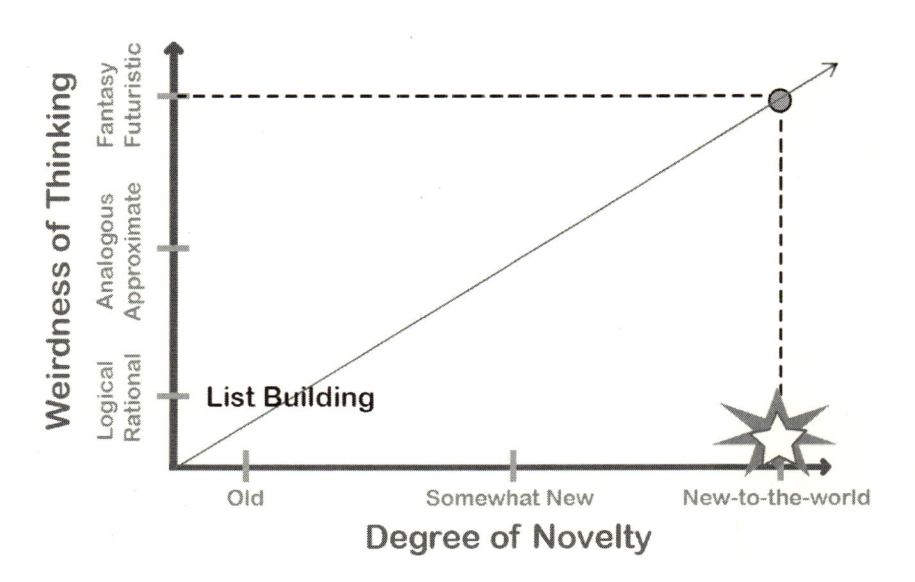

- <u>Verbal Instructions</u>: "Let's build a list of things that are efficient. Everyone just shout out an answer."

- <u>Answers may include things like:</u> assembly lines, daily planners, calendars, UPS, online searches, Amazon Prime delivery, self-checkout lines at the grocery, flow charts, one-click pay, smartphones, drive-through restaurants, etc.

- <u>Write each answer</u> on the flip chart, in the exact words of the participant sharing the idea—no editing!

- <u>Final Instructions</u>: "Look at this list of efficient things and use anything on it as inspiration for creating a new idea to increase our efficiency." Then, be silent and let the room incubate.

- <u>Collect new ideas:</u> Write them on the flip chart. For example, one idea might be, "Let's put every task into a flow chart and divide all tasks to create an assembly line of work flow."

2. Three Lists or "Triangle Exercise": This is also very easy because it's a variation on list-building. Use this excursion when there are several factors at play within your problem. This excursion goes just above list-building on the vertical axis of our chart. Let's assume we're still working on the problem of how to make my business more efficient.

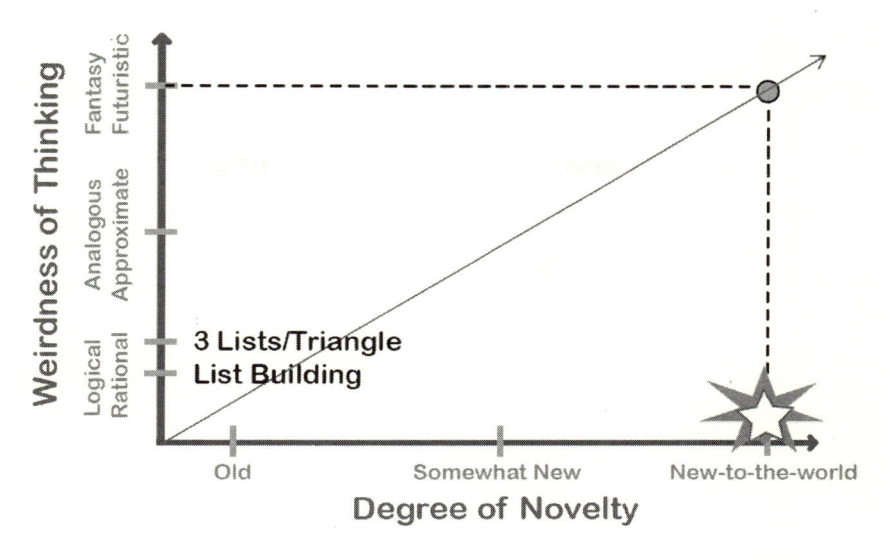

Weirdness of Thinking: Fantasy/Futuristic, Analogous/Approximate, Logical/Rational

3 Lists/Triangle List Building

Degree of Novelty: Old, Somewhat New, New-to-the-world

- Verbal Instructions are: "First shout out a list of our company's core competencies."

- Answers may include responses like: "Our product formulas, our proprietary production process, our efficient logistics, our reputation for being a great place to work, our ability to get the best out of our people."

- Write each answer on the flip chart.

- Repeat the process and record a list of things that are efficient on flip chart #2; then make a list of all our divisions and departments and record it on flip chart #3.

- Final Instructions: "Write down ONE WORD from each list—quickly." Take five seconds for List #1; then, take the list down and repeat with lists #2 and #3. "Next, look at the three words you wrote on your paper and force fit them together to create a new efficiency idea for one of our divisions/departments."

- Ask for silence and incubation time.

- Collect new ideas and write them on the flip chart. For example, if the three words I wrote were "production process" (competency), "UPS" (something efficient) and "Industrial Division" (our departments) a new idea might be, "Minimize inventory and eliminate need for storage with just-in-time production and shipping to our industrial clients; use the resulting space no longer needed for inventory storage to build new production lines."

- VARIATION on this exercise: The Triangle Exercise is a quiet activity that can be substituted for the "shout out three lists" version above. Use this variation when energy in the room is high and you want to regain control of the process. It also works well when your group—a room of artists or graphic designers, for example—is particularly visual.

    - Instead of writing three full lists, use the following instructions:
    - "Please take out a clean sheet of paper." [Wait until everyone has done this.]
    - "Draw a large triangle in the center of the page." [Wait until the task is completed.]
    - "On the first corner, write down ONE of our company's core competencies." [Again, wait.]
    - "On the second corner, write down ONE thing that is efficient—outside our company" [Wait.]
    - In the last corner, write down ONE of our divisions or departments." [Wait.]
    - Final instruction: "Use all three words as inspiration to create a new idea for making our company more efficient. Write your new idea in the middle of the

triangle."

The three items listed here are just examples that would work well to address an efficiency problem. If your problem is finding new ways to promote your product, your three lists might include: 1) our product's key attributes; 2) types of promotions; and 3) types of consumers who enjoy this product. The trick is to find three different things relevant to your problem that, when pulled together, create a comprehensive idea.

3. Word Association Clusters and Chains: This is also pretty easy to do and works very well for linear thinkers. Use word association clusters when you want to stay close in with your ideas—when you're improving an existing product, service or package, for example. Use Word Association Chains when you want to push your group to think more expansively to solve a tougher problem.

We will address Clusters first.

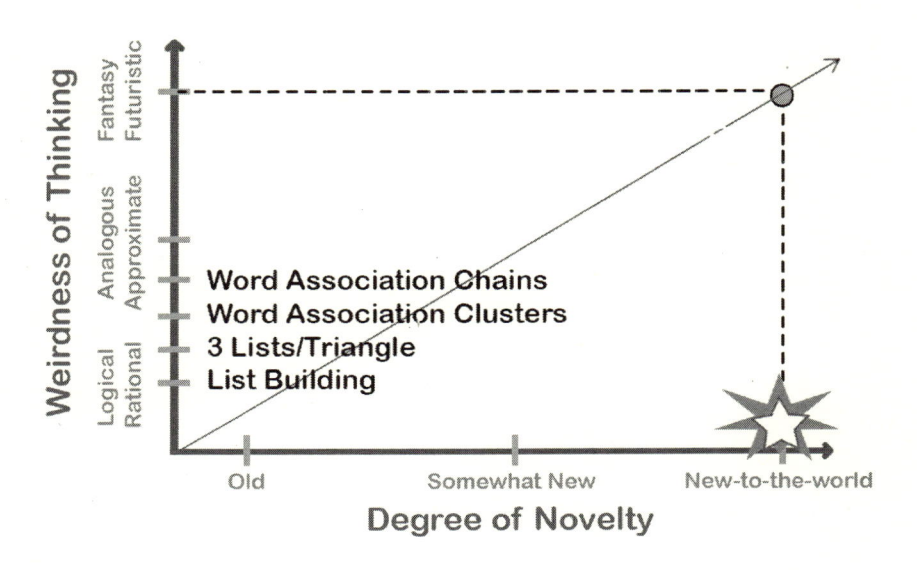

Chart: Weirdness of Thinking (Logical/Rational, Analogous/Approximate, Fantasy/Futuristic) vs. Degree of Novelty (Old, Somewhat New, New-to-the-world), showing techniques plotted along a diagonal: List Building, 3 Lists/Triangle, Word Association Clusters, Word Association Chains.

95

- Verbal Instructions are: "In the middle of your page, write down the word 'efficiency.'" [Wait.] "Then, draw several spokes around that word." [Wait.] "Now fill those spokes with ANYTHING at all that you ASSOCIATE with 'efficiency.' Keep going until all your spokes are filled."

- Answers may include responses like: "My mother in the kitchen, speed, high priority things first, technology, minimal steps, shorthand commands, one-click ordering" etc. All of these items are free associations and won't always make sense together. That's ok.

- Final Instructions: "Use your cluster of associations to come up with a new idea for making our business more efficient." Then call for silence and incubation time.

- Collect new ideas and write them on the flip chart. For example, the words above make me think of this new idea-- "Computerize as many internal processes as we can to reduce human error and increase speed of our work."

- VARIATION on this exercise: A word association chain can be a quiet activity done on each individual's notepad. It can also be used to energize your group by moving around the circle and having each individual stand up when he adds a word. A chain differs from a cluster in that each new word is an association with THE LAST WORD SAID, so we quickly veer away from the topic.

    o Ask participant #1 to say a word they associate with efficiency, such as "computer."

    o Participant #2 must think of a word they associate with "computer," such as "mouse."

- Participant #3 associates off of the word "mouse" with a word like "cheese." Keep going until you have at least ten different words. For example, your association chain might be: efficiency, computer, mouse, cheese, smelly, feet, run, exercise, heart rate, doctor.

- "Take ONLY the last six words, beginning with 'smelly,' and use them as inspiration to come up with a new idea for making our business more efficient."

- Then ask for silence and incubation time.

- Next, collect the new ideas on your flip chart. From the word "heart-rate" an idea like this might emerge: Increase speed of our production line carefully and incrementally, to get more product out in less time without experiencing quality problems.

APPROXIMATE THINKING/ANALOGOUS THINKING EXCURSIONS

As we begin to move up the vertical axis we enter the middle area of "analogous thinking" or "approximate thinking," which is really about playing in the world of metaphors. These exercises are a bit more difficult to use, especially for a group of linear thinkers. That's why it is particularly important to give your instructions one step at a time, and then wait for the group to complete the step before giving the next instruction.

1. **Role Play** is about taking a metaphorical walk in someone else's shoes and it offers a very easy way to change your perspective on a problem. There are several ways to role play including:
   a. Become your product.
   b. Become your target audience.
   c. Become your prospect.
   d. Become a cartoon or pop culture character.

Use the first three versions for closer-in problems, and the character role play to stretch your thinking. We will explain them in order.

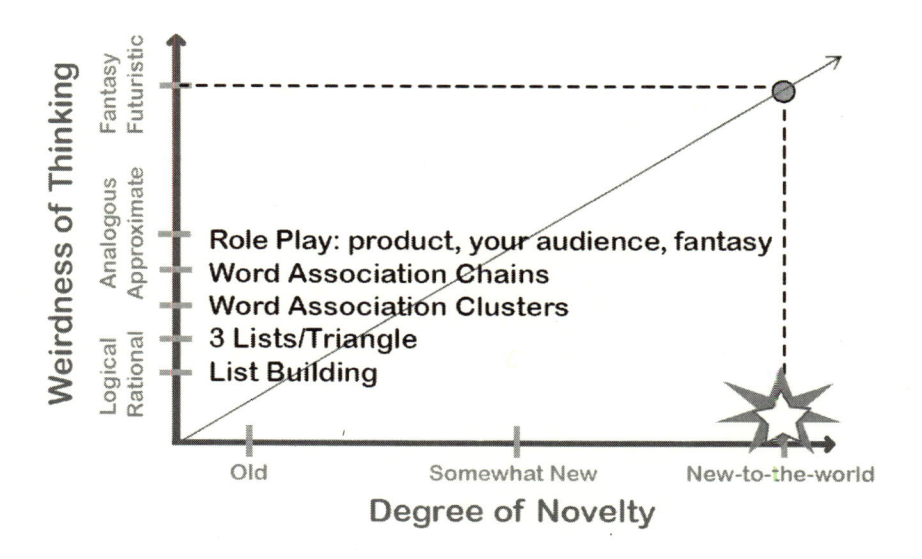

[Chart: Weirdness of Thinking (Logical/Rational, Analogous/Approximate, Fantasy/Futuristic) vs. Degree of Novelty (Old, Somewhat New, New-to-the-world). Items listed: Role Play: product, your audience, fantasy; Word Association Chains; Word Association Clusters; 3 Lists/Triangle; List Building]

1a) Product Role Play: Become Your Product

The product role play is an excellent exercise to use when you are trying to create many different options for product improvement. While helpful for incremental changes, it's not the best option to use when you really need to stretch yourself into new-to-the-world ideas. Here's how to do it.

- <u>Verbal Instructions are</u>: "Imagine for a moment you are part of our product." Call on people one at a time and assign them ONE ASPECT of your product. For example, if you're working with a bathroom fixtures company that's trying to improve the bathtub, you could assign one person to be each part: the left wall, the right wall, the front wall, the back wall, the drain, the faucet, the shower head, the shower curtain, etc.

- Then assign one person to be the end user or, in this example, the bather. Those representing aspects of the tub can come to the front of the room and stand together in a way that "builds" the product in front of the team's eyes. Have the bather step in, go through the motions of a shower or bath and get out, while the rest of the group concentrates on what it's like to be their roles — the side of the tub, the drain, etc.

- Send everyone back to their seats with the instruction, "Make notes of what you –in your role as a bathtub part-- want that will make yourself even better." [Wait.]

- <u>Answers may include responses like</u>: "As the side of the tub I want to be softer, more luxurious feeling; I want to be special and noticed; I want to embrace the bather in a feeling of joy" etc.

- <u>Final Instructions:</u> "Then use your notes to create product improvement ideas for your portion of the bathtub."

- <u>Ask for silence</u> and incubation time.

- <u>Collect new ideas</u> and write them on the flip chart. For example, my notes on being the side of the bathtub led me

99

to the new idea, "cushiony material, a la memory foam that is non-porous enough to stay clean but also gives way for luxurious comfort."

1b) Consumer/Customer Role Play: Become Your Target Audience

Still focusing on the example of new innovations for bathroom fixtures, let's look at how we might conduct a target audience role play exercise to create better bathtubs. This role play works great when you find your team is becoming a bit too myopic — at that point participants need to immerse themselves in their customers' mindset. Here's how you do it.

- Verbal Instructions are: "Forget about our topic for a moment and imagine you are one of the businesses we sell to." Call on people one at a time and assign them ONE TYPE of business customer. For example, customer types for a bathroom fixtures company might include fixture distributors, large construction companies, private home builders, top designers, hotel chains, etc.

- Continue with instructions by saying, "Think about who you are and make detailed notes about yourself on your notepad. Write down what is important to you in your life as this customer." [Wait.] "Now add some notes about who are the important people in your life. [Wait.] "What are your hopes and dreams?" [Wait.] "What are your pet peeves?" Now wait about 60 more seconds and allow people to write.

- Answers may include responses like: "As a top designer, I work hard to build my reputation as a visionary who is easy to work with. I am always looking for the next great thing to show my clients. I have a reputation for always knowing about the latest and greatest and I love to make a statement with my work. My important people are: my spouse, who supports my efforts and brings in a steady income so I can do project work; my assistant, who has a great eye for beauty and practicality; and my children, who look to me as a role model. My hopes and dreams include building an ongoing design business that my children can take over. My pet peeves include clients who can't visualize and/or micromanage without any knowledge."

- Final Instructions: "Then use anything at all you have written in your notes to create new product ideas for next generation bathtubs. Be sure to use your notes only as inspiration and create an idea *everyone* would like, beyond just your assigned target audience."

- Ask for silence and allow incubation time.

- Collect new ideas and write them on the flip chart. They might include a bathtub with remarkable features like a cutting-edge appearance, ergonomic design for the ultimate in comfort and new highly durable materials like titanium, for durability and a futuristic look.

- VARIATION on Consumer/Customer Role Play: Another fun way to truly get into the minds of your target consumer or customer is to role play a common conflict, sitting in pairs around the room so no one is "performing" in front of the entire team. When one person is talking, the other is making notes; then switch and have the other person speak while the partner takes notes. Have both discuss themselves in their roles, or the situation. Interesting role play combinations include:

- A parent and child arguing over whether to buy a certain product

- A customer and your internal sales professional discussing his needs and your products

- Two friends discussing the benefits of a product or service from two different perspectives

Several other options may be relevant to your own business or company culture. If you use this technique the instructions are a bit different from the Product Role Play instructions:

- "Discuss the issue you have been assigned, with the listener making detailed notes of the speaker's comments. {Wait 3 minutes.]

- "Now switch, and let your partner speak, while the new listener makes detailed notes." {Wait 3 minutes.]

- "Now, work together and use your discussion and notes as inspiration for a new product or service that appeals to both roles and solves this conflict." [Wait 3-5 minutes.]

- Then collect ideas.

1c) Fantasy Role Play: Become a Cartoon or Pop Culture Character

Still focusing on the example of new innovations for bathroom fixtures, let's look at how we might conduct a cartoon character or pop-culture character role play to create better bathtubs. When you need truly breakthrough ideas no one else has ever thought of, this exercise works well because it can yield futuristic, new-to-the-world ideas that are tough to elicit using closer-in techniques. Here is how you do it.

- <u>Verbal Instructions are:</u> "Forget about our topic for a moment and imagine you are a specific character—from a cartoon, pop culture or history." Call on people one at a time and assign them ONE character from either a cartoon or current pop culture—such as SpongeBob Squarepants, Lady Gaga, Abraham Lincoln, Bill O'Reilly, Batman, The Cake Boss, Princess Leia, Elsa from Frozen, a current meme, Justin Bieber, a controversial political figure, etc. Regardless of your topic, make your character selections at random and mix them up.

- Then give the same instructions listed in **1b) target audience role play** and say, "Think about who you are and make detailed notes about yourself on your notepad. Write down what is important to you in your life as this character." [Wait.] "Now add some notes about the important people in your life. [Wait.] "What are your hopes and dreams?" [Wait.] "What are your pet peeves?" [Wait about 60 more seconds and allow people to write.]

- <u>Answers may include responses like:</u> "As Abe Lincoln, I work hard to do what's right, despite a lot of opposition. I love to discuss the high ideals of our great nation. I feel comfortable making the tough decisions. My wife, Mary Todd, and my sons are very important to me, which is why I work so hard to make the world a better place. I dislike treachery and dishonesty, and I hope for a better, more egalitarian world."

- <u>Final Instructions</u>: "Then use anything you have written in your notes to create new product ideas for next generation bathtubs. Be sure to use your notes only as inspiration and create a mainstream idea everyone would like, not just your specific character."

- <u>Ask for silence</u> and allow incubation time.

- <u>Collect new ideas</u> and write them on a flip chart. These might include a classic claw-foot bathtub with modern features like water conservation flow inhibitors, a water quality gauge, water temperature gauges and a self-warming feature to keep water at a constant temperature.

2. **The Random Object Excursion** is not difficult to do and most people find it fun, including linear thinkers. It involves—literally—finding any object and force-fitting it to your problem to create a new idea. Here is where it sits on our Excursion Chart.

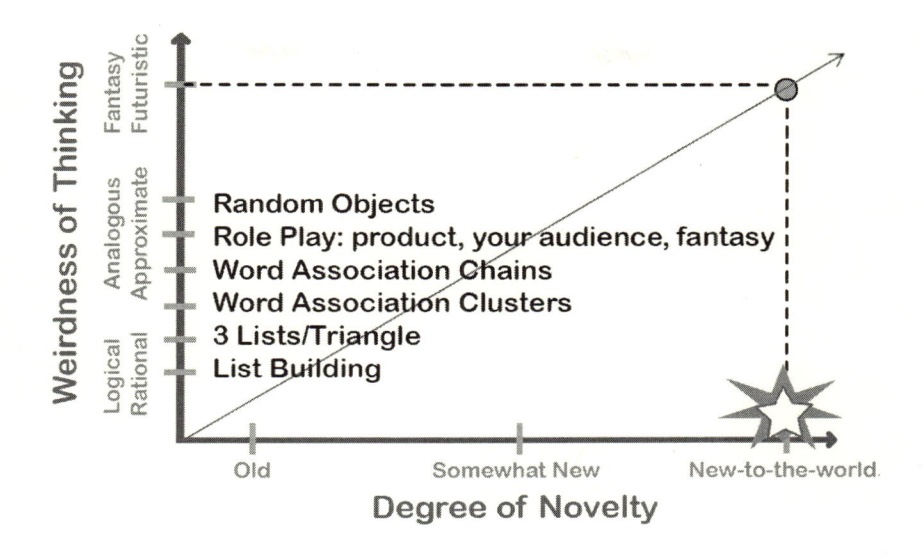

Weirdness of Thinking (y-axis, from bottom to top): Logical/Rational, Analogous/Approximate, Fantasy/Futuristic

- Random Objects
- Role Play: product, your audience, fantasy
- Word Association Chains
- Word Association Clusters
- 3 Lists/Triangle
- List Building

Degree of Novelty (x-axis): Old, Somewhat New, New-to-the-world

You can choose one of several ways to do this:

a. Simply look around the room you're in and name an object you see, e.g. a hole in the wall where a nail used to be.

b. In advance, use a brown paper bag or other opaque container to create a grab bag of small but diverse objects you have collected (e.g., a Barbie shoe, golf tee, eraser, can pop top, Phillips head screw, etc.)

c. As homework, ask your participants to gather and bring in random household objects from their homes: a spatula, pencil sharpener, button, spare change, piece of junk mail, nail file, etc.

d. Ask your participants to reach into their wallet, purse, computer bag or backpack and pull out the first thing they touch. This could be a receipt, dollar bill, Chap Stick, paper clip, a mint, etc.

   e. Ask the team to imagine they just opened a junk drawer at home; what would they find in there? Items might include a tape measure, scissors, 3 x 5 notecard, twist ties, etc.

- <u>Verbal Instructions are:</u> "Forget about our topic for a moment and find any random object. Write it down on your notepad." [Wait.] "Now force fit your object to our problem to create a new product for bathtubs." Wait and allow incubation time.

- <u>Answers may include responses like</u>:

   - Nail hole + bathtub = tub with tiny holes lining the bottom that open to drain five times faster than an average drain.

   - Stapler + bathtub = flip top tub that always contains water at the right temperature to provide a hot tub experience in the house.

   - Barbie shoe + bathtub = hot pink sparkly mini-bathtub for little girls' bathrooms in luxury homes; black sparkly "outer-space" version for boys.

   - Spatula + bathtub = a tub with a series of paddles you can move and reposition to create a unique, targeted jet for achy muscles.

   - Receipt + bathtub = data connection to your smartphone that records all relevant information, warns you if water is too hot or too deep for a toddler, increases temperature slightly over time to keep water warm, reports bacteria level, etc.

- Tape measure + bathtub = measuring unit on the side of tub and shower that lets you know how much water you've used over the course of a month.

- Write new ideas on a flip chart.

3. The Visual Stimulus Excursion is a great tool to use when you have a lot of visual thinkers. You can identify visual thinkers by listening to how they speak. For example, they say things like, "I see" in response to information, and use other visual language such as, "I'm envisioning a solution that . . ." or "What does that look like?" when they want more information.

The technique itself is simple: Choose any image and force fit it to our problem to create a new idea by saying, "Use this picture as inspiration to come up with a new idea for _____."

Here is where it sits on our Excursion Chart:

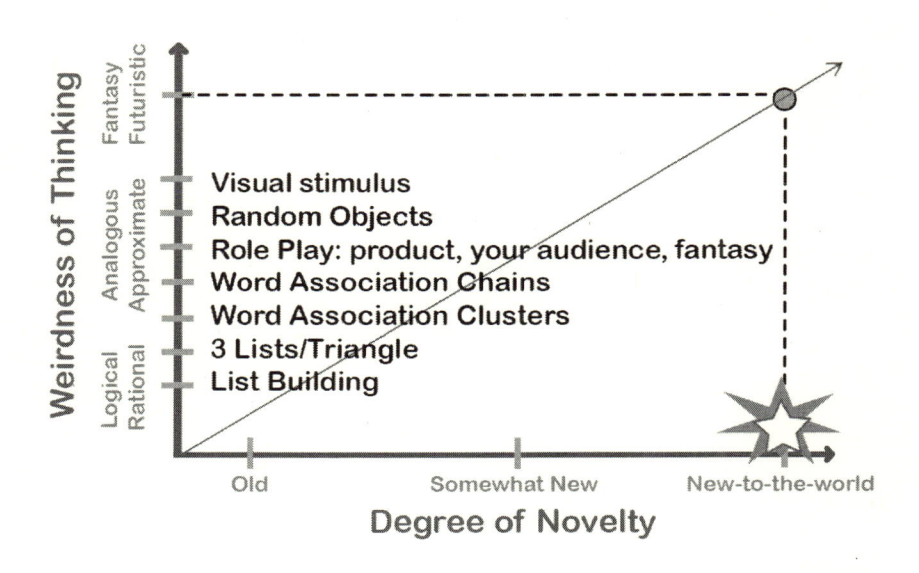

Weirdness of Thinking (y-axis, from bottom to top): Logical/Rational, Analogous/Approximate, Fantasy/Futuristic

- Visual stimulus
- Random Objects
- Role Play: product, your audience, fantasy
- Word Association Chains
- Word Association Clusters
- 3 Lists/Triangle
- List Building

Degree of Novelty (x-axis): Old, Somewhat New, New-to-the-world

There are several ways to do this:

   a. Picture cards - Many decks exist with a different image on every card. Try "Eames House of Cards" or something similar. Just have each participant pick a card and force fit it to the problem.

   b. Environment pictures - Flip through magazines or catalogs and tear out photos that evoke different environments: a beach photo, a cigar club interior, a street fair, classroom, mountains, yachts, academia, an African street scene, etc. Go for diversity. Then ask every participant to grab any photo and force fit it to the problem.

   c. Draw and pass - Try this version when you need a change of pace. Ask everyone to get a clean piece of paper. [Wait.] Then have them draw one large numeral from 0-9 on the page. [Wait.] Next, have them rip it off and pass it to the person to their right. [Wait.] Instruct them to take the paper they have been given and add a line or doodle" [Wait.] Have them pass again to the right.

   Keep going in this way until all participants get their original papers back. Then, ask them to look into the resulting composite drawing for anything that inspires an idea to address the purpose.

d. Sculpture - Pass out pipe cleaners or chenille sticks (the politically correct term for pipe cleaner these days, or so I'm told.) Put participants in teams of two and say, "Use your craft supplies to build a sculpture together — it can be anything at all or nothing in particular." [Wait at least three to four minutes for them to complete this activity.] Then say, "Now look at your sculpture and use anything in it as inspiration for a new idea that solves our problem."

- Answers may include responses like: Swirls on my sculpture + bathtub = tub for kid's bathroom with a small curly slide to get them in and out easily and in a fun way.

- Write new ideas on a flip chart.

4. Get Fired Idea or Take it to the Extreme is a great way to get a corporate group to think way, way outside the box. It's all about finding a truly horrendous idea, one that would presumably get you fired if you became the advocate for the idea. It seems that horrendous ideas tend to flow freely, but "good" ideas are nearly impossible to come up with. Go figure.

Here is where this technique fits on our Excursions Chart:

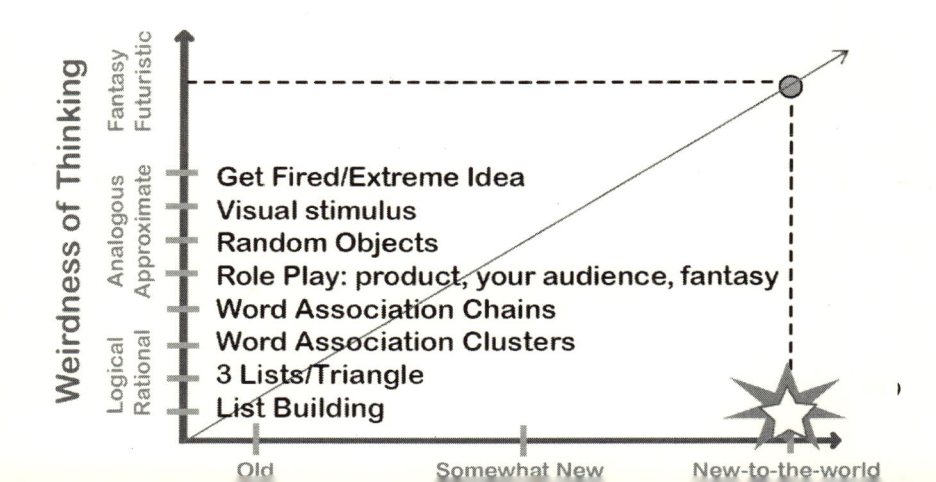

Weirdness of Thinking (Logical/Rational → Analogous/Approximate → Fantasy/Futuristic)

- Get Fired/Extreme Idea
- Visual stimulus
- Random Objects
- Role Play: product, your audience, fantasy
- Word Association Chains
- Word Association Clusters
- 3 Lists/Triangle
- List Building

Old — Somewhat New — New-to-the-world

Still focusing on the example of new innovations for bathroom fixtures, let's look at how we might conduct the Get Fired exercise to create new product ideas. To make it a bit more fun, let's add that we want this tub to be the ultimate in comfort. Here is how you do it.

- <u>Verbal Instructions are</u>: "Forget about our topic for a moment. Everyone please get a clean piece of paper. Anywhere on your paper, I want you to write the worst possible idea you can think of. This is the most uncomfortable bathtub imaginable. Feel free to defy the laws of our land, the laws of physics, any ethical considerations—everything. Go wild on this idea!" [Wait until everyone has written an idea. You will hear some chuckles around the room.]

- Now have everyone trade papers with the person next to them. If you have an odd number of participants you can instead have everyone pass the bad idea to the person on their right.

- <u>Bad ideas may include responses like:</u> a tub with metal spikes sticking into you from all sides; a tub that has been chemically treated with cocaine so you soak and feel numb; a tub with torture attachments that creates a personalized torture routine for anyone who gets into it.

- <u>Final Instructions</u>: "Now use your bad idea as inspiration for a new bathtub that provides the ultimate in comfort."

- <u>Ask for silence</u> and incubation time.

- <u>Write new ideas</u> on a flip chart - Jumping off the "spikes" idea, a comfort version includes a bathtub with tiny acupuncture points that feel great when you lie in the tub the right way, eliminating aches and pains, headaches, backaches, etc.

One Final Tip with this technique: Unlike other techniques where we skip the back story and get right to the headline of the idea, it's very energizing to report out the bad idea first and then the good idea, as it creates a lot of laughter and also gives a rich context to the good idea.

5. The Worlds Excursion is a powerful brainstorming tool that yields very practical and breakthrough ideas because it leverages the power of analogies. This technique is more complicated to lead than some of the others, but if you use it at the right time, profound things can happen.

Here is where it sits on our Excursion Chart:

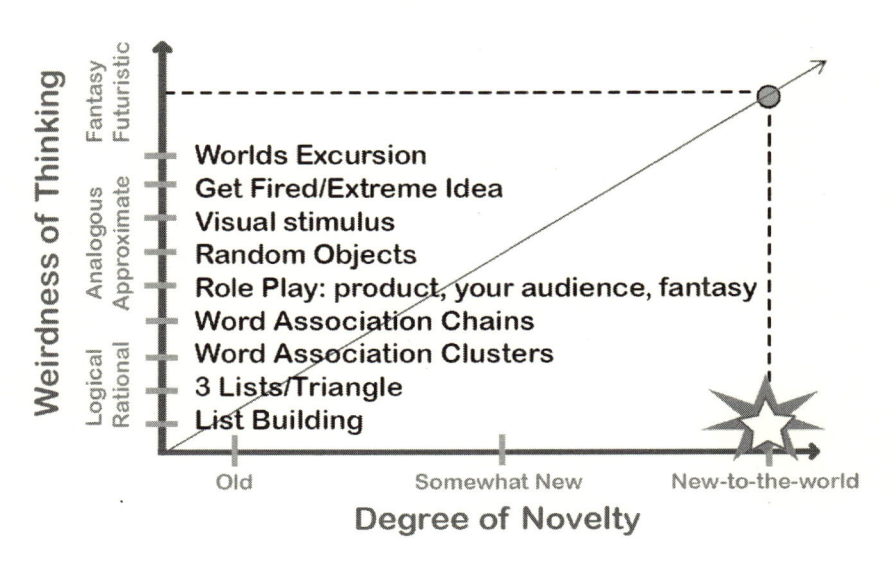

```
Weirdness of Thinking
  Fantasy/Futuristic    — Worlds Excursion
                        — Get Fired/Extreme Idea
  Analogous/Approximate — Visual stimulus
                        — Random Objects
                        — Role Play: product, your audience, fantasy
                        — Word Association Chains
                        — Word Association Clusters
  Logical/Rational      — 3 Lists/Triangle
                        — List Building
                        
              Old    Somewhat New    New-to-the-world
                    Degree of Novelty
```

Still focusing on the example of new innovations for bathroom fixtures, let's look at how we might conduct a Worlds Excursions

111

to create new product ideas for ultimate-comfort bathtubs. Here is how you do it.

- Verbal Instructions are: "Forget about our topic for a moment. I am going to assign you a 'world' and within your world I want you to quickly find an example of 'comfort.' Don't over-think it." Then assign each person one world to mentally "visit" such as the circus, deep sea, high fashion, espionage, children's literature, space exploration, costume design, personal care, rap music, politics, cartoons, senior citizens, baby care, rock bands, etc.

- Call on each person individually and ask, "What is your example of comfort?" Then—and this is the harder part—ask them HOW their example delivers comfort. On the left side of your flip chart record the example (NOT the world itself). On the right side of your flip chart, record "how" comfort is delivered.

- Answers may include responses like: Inner air conditioning, for an example of "comfort" in the world of costume design—this delivers comfort (the HOW) with a fan that moves air around. So you write down "costume air conditioning" on the left side of the flip chart; and then "fan moves air" on the right side of the chart.

An example of comfort in the deep sea might be bobbing ocean waves lulling me to sleep, which delivers comfort by gently rocking me back and forth. So you would write down, "bobbing waves" on the left, and "rocking me to sleep" on the right side.

In the world of espionage, an example of comfort might be "knowing I am safe and secure." HOW it delivers comfort is the feelings of relaxation and peace. So you write down on the left, "knowing I'm safe/secure" and on the right side, write, "feelings of relaxation and peace."

- <u>Final Instructions:</u> "Now use anything on this list as inspiration for a new bathtub that provides the ultimate in comfort."

- <u>Ask for silence</u> and incubation time.

- <u>Write new ideas</u> on a flip chart - The list might include a bathtub that sways back and forth to rock you gently in the water. Or a bathtub made completely of non-slip materials to keep you safe and secure.

FANTASY EXCURSIONS

These excursions are the most powerful and also the scariest. Use them when you truly want big change. But before I explain how to do these, a word of caution is warranted.

Over the course of my career in innovation, many clients have brought us in to bring about "real and lasting change" or "step-change innovation." During those years I have learned that my idea of what those terms mean may be much different than how my clients define them.

I experienced this, for example, when I worked with a quick service restaurant that had a long and positive history in the U.S. Here's what happened:

The company hired us in 2010 to lead the team in a session to "totally rethink the business" for the purpose of revitalizing it and sustainably distinguishing the company from its competitors. Because of its history, the company had a lot of positive brand equity, all of which was closely tied to the heartstrings of customers—most of America grew up on its delicious food and felt nostalgic whenever they came across the brand.

This is a rare and wonderful place for a company to be—a key piece of Americana that evokes innocent and happy memories of past visits and simpler times and elicits warm feelings among customers as they drive by the company's sign! I saw a ton of opportunity to set them apart in a way no competitor could match.

As always, I used a series of questions to clarify the team's needs before jumping into the work. I asked, "Can we change the design of your restaurants in any way to create a different environment? Maybe restore your restaurants to their retro look?" The answer, of course, was "No." Then I asked, "Can we change the locations of any restaurants to adjust their image in the marketplace?" "No." "Can we change the advertising or signage in any way?" "No." "Can we change the menu items in any way?" "Maybe . . ."

In my mind, updating a few menu items in a restaurant did not constitute "totally rethinking the business." However, the seemingly small adjustment of a few menu items felt like radical change to the company. And their definition is the only one that matters.

Here is another great example:

I worked recently for a large consumer products manufacturer that created a new department called "Futuristic Innovation" The team was charged with creating "disruptive innovation" that would allow the company to reposition itself for the future, to break out of the "chemical" perception of its products and be more "natural," and to significantly increase its appeal to Millennial parents.

The person who hired me was a brilliant man with excellent experience—a future-focused leader who was very open in his thinking and had a great title: Wizard of Future Innovation! I was very excited to have the opportunity to really stretch and come up with solutions that could completely reimagine the future of the company and ensure it would be poised to thrive for the next 100 years.

However, when I began asking questions to understand the manager's goals and challenges, it quickly became clear that he had merely been charged with finding more ways to use existing production lines, existing raw ingredients and existing packaging configurations. There was nothing "wizardly" or "futuristic" about what turned out to be simply a cost-savings and efficiency effort, dressed up in "futuristic" clothing.

What's the moral of the story? Always understand your client's definition of "innovation" or their definition of their "problem" to be solved. If they don't want to stretch, nothing you do will convince them to take the risk. Some companies are so rule-bound that an idea like changing the color of the label on their package is considered too risky to say out loud. Everyone has a different tolerance for risk.

With that said, let's jump into a discussion of fantasy excursions. These techniques are all about pure imagination.

1. LEGO® Projective Technique: This activity can be done as a group. It's fun to play with LEGOs®, and even more fun when you can find profound truths and big ideas while playing. For this exercise, everyone gets an identical cellophane bag of mixed LEGO pieces. Here is where it falls on our chart.

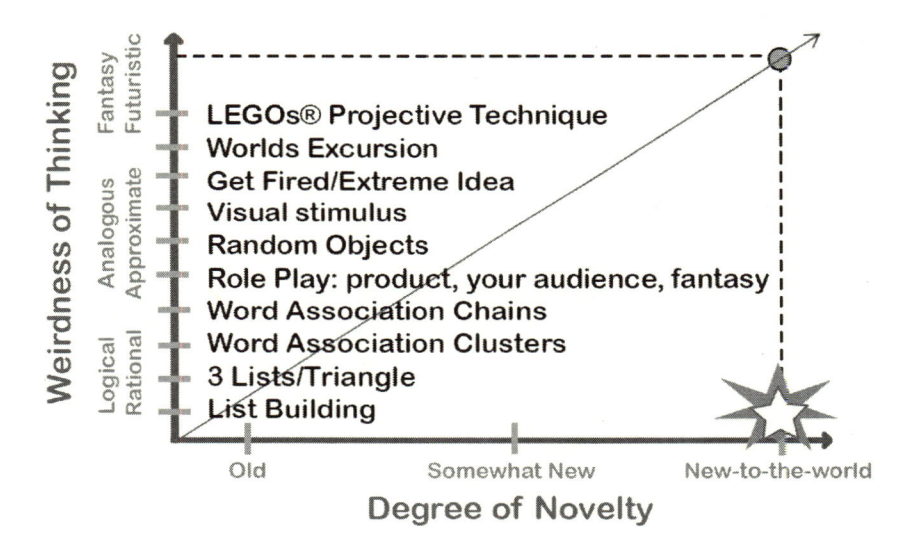

Chart: Weirdness of Thinking (Logical/Rational, Analogous/Approximate, Fantasy/Futuristic) vs. Degree of Novelty (Old, Somewhat New, New-to-the-world). Items listed from top to bottom: LEGOs® Projective Technique, Worlds Excursion, Get Fired/Extreme Idea, Visual stimulus, Random Objects, Role Play: product, your audience, fantasy, Word Association Chains, Word Association Clusters, 3 Lists/Triangle, List Building.

- <u>Verbal Instructions are:</u> "Our topic is bathtubs that are the ultimate in comfort. Now, please forget about our topic. In a moment, I am going to ask you to please open your LEGO bags, and pour out the pieces. Ok, please open your bags. [Wait.] "Take your pieces and create a "castle" called 'comfort,' making sure to build in all kinds of comfortable features." Allow five full minutes for each person to build a castle.

- Then, quiet the room and say, "Stop. Whatever you have now is great. Next, when I say 'go' please start with one person at your table who will explain all the comfort features in the castle; the person to their right will make notes of what the speaker says." [Wait.]

- "Now, I would like the rest of the group at each table to ask the first speaker questions about additional features by posing the question, 'Tell me about this element.' For each question, allow the speaker to elaborate on the UNCONSCIOUS elements of comfort he built into his castle, but wasn't aware he added them." [Wait.] Then say, "Time for the next speaker to show his Comfort Castle."

- Do this 8 times if there are 8 people per table. Make sure everyone gets the same chance to share ideas.

- The power of this exercise comes from drawing out the unconscious elements that create comfort without the builder being aware they are there. This is what makes this technique "projective."

- <u>Castle descriptions may include responses like:</u> "These steps are mini-cushions that move by themselves to transport you anywhere by floating in the air. There are bobbing marshmallow stepping stones across the moat that your feet sink into to help you grip. The windows are made of sheer satin fabric that softens sunlight and lets air flow through. This room is for rest; this room is for massages; this room is for comfort food meals; this room is for sauna; this room is for steam; this room is for a hot or cold tub," etc.

- Team questions may include responses like: "tell me about the drawbridge" and the speaker makes up comfort-related answers like, "the drawbridge is pulled up by satin tassels, and it has hydraulics so it takes no effort to pull it."

- Final Instructions: "Now use any part of the notes or discussion to generate ideas for a bathtub that is the ultimate in comfort."

- Ask for silence and incubation time.

- Write new ideas on a flip chart - For this topic, ideas might include an outdoor bathtub-shower-hot tub-sauna-steam room combo with soft jets everywhere and cushioned surfaces, plus underwater music tied to a music streaming service. The unit adjusts effortlessly with hydraulics.

2. Guided Imagery - This is an individual activity in which participants use their own imaginations and make their own notes of the experience. Here is where this technique fits on our chart:

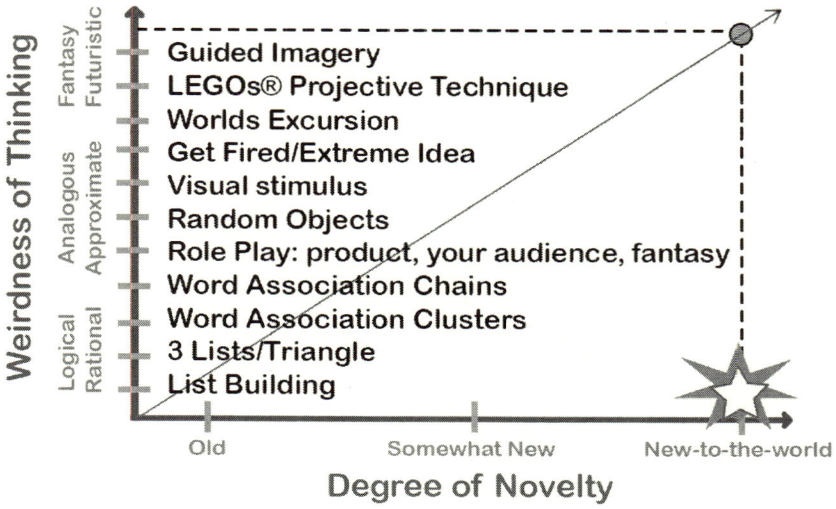

Weirdness of Thinking
Fantasy Futuristic
Analogous Approximate
Logical Rational
Guided Imagery
LEGOs® Projective Technique
Worlds Excursion
Get Fired/Extreme Idea
Visual stimulus
Random Objects
Role Play: product, your audience, fantasy
Word Association Chains
Word Association Clusters
3 Lists/Triangle
List Building
Old
Somewhat New
New-to-the-world
Degree of Novelty

- <u>Verbal Instructions are:</u> "Forget about our topic for a moment. I am going to ask everyone to please close their eyes and get comfortable in your seats." [Wait.] Then speak softly and take everyone through a brief relaxation exercise. "Now I want you to relax. Start at your head and move slowly down to your feet, to relax every part of your body. Let it melt into your chair. First relax your facial muscles....[wait]...then your neck muscles... [wait]...then your shoulder muscles...etc." until you get all the way down to their toes. Then pause for a moment.

- Once everyone is relaxed, slowly tell a futuristic story in a soft and soothing voice. Here is one that works well:

- "Imagine you are getting ready to go to sleep in your home tonight. You drop off to sleep easily and peacefully, and wake up feeling wonderful. But as soon as you wake up, you realize everything is different. You've slept for 500 years and have woken up to a whole new world. Look around your room. Wow! How it's changed! What do you see?" [Wait.] "How does that make you feel?" [Wait.]

"Now your curiosity is really piqued so you go to the window, open it up and stick your head out so you can see all around you. How radical the future is! Nothing is as it was! What do you see as you look around?" [Wait.] "Look up...what do you see?"[Wait.] "Look to the right—what do you see?" [Wait.] "Look to your left—what do you see?" [Wait.] "Look down—what do you see?" [Wait a final 20 seconds or so.]

Then say, "Slowly, when you're ready, please open your eyes" [Wait until everyone has done so]. "Now, use your notepad to make detailed notes of what you experienced, what you saw, what you felt, what you heard, and what you thought as you lived in the future."

- <u>Answers may include responses like:</u> "I saw shoe jets and gyrocopters flying everyone around individually. I saw treadmill paths in my home for extra exercise. I saw artificial nature everywhere—fake grass, trees, flowers, etc."

- <u>Final Instructions</u>: "Now use anything in your notes as inspiration for a new futuristic bathtub."

- <u>Ask for silence</u> and incubation time.

- <u>Write new ideas</u> on a flip chart – For example, a bathtub over an air pocket (like a hovercraft or air hockey) so it floats and bobs magically in the air. When you get in, the easy motion feels wonderful. It also contains strong front jets so you can "swim laps" in it like a treadmill tub.

To summarize, there are many, many different tools and techniques that will stretch your own and your team's thinking. Once you become accustomed to using these tools, you will find you can easily invent other excursions to get you where you need to go. The key is to find tools that have many diverse elements—like lots of different words, lots of different pictures, etc.

Here are some great examples:

- Don't like chenille sticks? Make Play-Doh or clay sculptures and dig into them for ideas.

- Do you love Trivial Pursuit? Use the cards that come in the pack as a pick-a-card exercise. Each card contains many different words that will trigger a range of thinking.

- Working on real estate and mortgage innovation? Pull the housing cards from the Game of Life to trigger thinking about different types of home purchases, life stages, and geographic needs.

- Hate collages? Instead, ask people to use any medium to make an artistic expression of the topic (for example, a poem about cheese). This can be a short story, original cartoon, ballad or Rap, a painting or drawing, a costume, a diorama, a board game representing the customer's journey or company challenge, etc. All of these are powerful variations on the tried-and-true collage.

- Do you enjoy the popular games *Apples to Apples*? The game has a large card deck with adjectives and a few corresponding synonyms on each card. What better way is there to apply new qualities to a product or service to make it better? For example, how can we make natural cheese "memorable?" Or how can we make cheese "edgy?" How can we make it "nostalgic?" All of these are great starting points for applying new qualities to your product or service.

A FEW WORDS ABOUT DATA AS AN EXCURSION TECHNIQUE

Many companies love to start their brainstorming process with data, to ensure the ideas are grounded in truths and to make sure the effort addresses true market needs. I am 100% in favor of this. However, using data dumps *during* brainstorming can be very, very difficult and incredibly frustrating because data alone do not trigger new ideas. It isn't until we play with the data, even a little bit, that ideas naturally emerge from an analysis.

Here's how it works: Let's imagine we are starting our bathtub new products session with a big review of "what we know", such as the history of tubs, improvements through the ages, current trends in the bathroom fixture industry, data on our sales versus our competitors' sales, customer complaint summaries, analyses of features and benefits in all the competitors' tubs and fixtures, advertising reels of all the bathroom fixture ads run since 1960, etc.

The facts themselves will only take you so far. However, when we use worksheets as we listen to all the facts, we can leverage the data in a way that makes new ideas obvious. The thinking process is as follows:

1. **What?** Write down the fact or data you just heard.

2. **So what?** Write down one key implication for your business.

3. **Now what?** Write down a new idea that addresses the business implication.

I frequently encourage clients to use the worksheet here as they are listening to presentations of data from their teammates. When they hear an interesting fact, they jot it down in the far left column. Then they deliberately stop listening to the meeting so they can think about what that fact means for the business and jot it down in the middle column. Still not listening to the meeting, they create a new idea and record it on the far right column. Then they turn their attention back to the meeting and listen in again until a new fact sparks for them. Then repeat.

Here is an example of how this sheet might be used by a bathroom fixtures company.

What? (Data)	So What? (Business Implications)	Now What? (New Idea)
Jets in tubs appeal to 83% of women 18-55, but only 27% find them affordable	Right now we only compete in the high end market, with tubs with jets that have cutting edge air flow technology. But we have nothing to offer budget customers	A budget line of jet tubs with fewer jets, basic technology; partner with large apartment construction companies or mid-tier hotels to offer a mutually beneficial "amenity" for tenants or guests
Another fact...		
Another fact...		

As you look at the example above, imagine trying to come up with that idea directly from the data. It would be relatively difficult because the part of your brain that creates new ideas is very different from the part that analyzes data. To come up with ideas you must pull your brain out of the facts and numbers in order to turn them into a concept of some sort that can be built upon and used.

WORKING WITH SWOTS

A very popular business analysis technique called "SWOT" is often done as a precursor to brainstorming. SWOT stands for:

- Strengths
- Weaknesses
- Opportunities
- Threats

To use a SWOT, managers look at their businesses from all angles and make long lists of facts and opinions that outline

123

what they're great at, what they're not so great at, new opportunities to grow, and threats to the future of the business.

Sometimes the analysis is backed by data and numbers, while at other times it's more qualitative in nature. Information that's already in qualitative or conceptual form (instead of a large table of numbers) can be a great idea trigger. For example, a company strength might be its state-of-the-art factories staffed with the best operations talent available in the world.

If you find that your SWOT analysis is filled with charts, statistics and numbers, we recommend using the data listening worksheets with the What?--So what?--Now what? format.

IN AND OUT LISTENING

Generating ideas within a group is a true team sport. Because we are all different, more people = richer results. But here is the rub: available airtime within a group is limited. If we have a four-hour meeting with 20 participants, each person only has up to 12 minutes each to speak during that four hours, assuming the leader never speaks. That's not much time at all, so we all have to share airtime.

To overcome this problem, you can limit the number of participants. In addition, you can use this handy technique called In-and-Out Listening.

Let me use a chart to explain how this works. In the diagram below, the vertical axis represents the percentage of your attention that you're giving to the meeting. The horizontal axis represents time—more specifically, how long the meeting lasts. At the beginning of a meeting everyone is at 100% attention. This is true especially during introductions because no one wants to repeat what another person said. At some point, however, it's inevitable that everyone will mentally drop out of even the most exciting and captivating meeting.

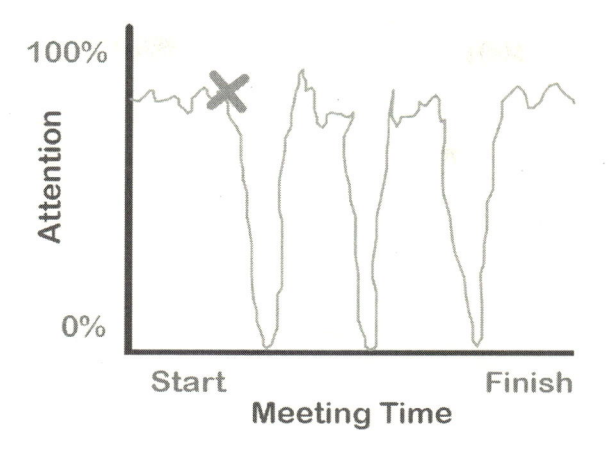

[Chart: Attention (0% to 100%) vs Meeting Time (Start to Finish), showing attention spiking high then dropping sharply multiple times, with an "X" marked at one of the high points.]

That's because when you hear something that triggers any intriguing idea, you mentally leave the meeting (indicated in the chart with an "X"). The trigger may be an idea contributed by a teammate that is on topic. But it is often something completely unrelated, such as, "Did I remember to put the laundry in the dryer before I left?" or "I wonder what they're serving for lunch." During brainstorming, this In and Out Listening is a great tool for finding useful ideas.

Here's how it works: Start by listening for anything that intrigues you for any reason. When that happens, stop listening and use the thought as inspiration to create a new idea. Once you get your new idea, write it down so you don't forget it. Then listen in again.

Don't worry about what you've missed when your head is "out" of the meeting, as your teammates are listening in and out the same way and are picking up on other tidbits that spark their own thinking. At first it may be difficult to permit yourself to stop listening because we've all been told from a very young age to "PAY ATTENTION!" Please force yourself to NOT listen intermittently throughout the meeting. If you are listening carefully 100% of the time, you are not creating anything new — that's guaranteed.

CHAPTER TEN SUMMARY – EXCURSION TOOLS AND TECHNIQUES

1. There are many, many different excursion exercises, all of which take you on a small "mental trip" to another arena, where you can find a relevant idea to borrow and apply to your problem.

2. Key techniques outlined here include a blend of verbal activities for verbal thinkers, visual activities for visual thinkers, kinesthetic activities for hands-on learners and projective techniques that reveal ideas you didn't know you had.

3. They include:
    - Attributes List
    - Associations List
    - 3 Lists or Triangle Exercise
    - Word Association Clusters and Chains
    - Role Play Many Different Ways
    - Random Objects
    - Visual Stimulus
    - Get Fired Idea/ Extreme Idea
    - Worlds Excursion
    - LEGOs® Projective Technique
    - Guided Imagery

4. Prepare many excursions in advance, and keep them all in your back pocket. Then choose your excursion in the moment, based on:
    a. Fit with the topic

    b.   Thinking styles of your participants
    c.   Energy level in the room
    d. How breakthrough the solution needs to be

5. Once you get some practice, make up your own excursions!

6. If you work with data, use a worksheet to extract new ideas-- What? So what? and Now what?

7. If you like to work with SWOTs, qualitative information can be used as-is to trigger ideas; if your SWOT is data-driven, use worksheets.

8. Practice In-and-Out listening when you work in a group.

TIPS FOR PERSONAL PROBLEM SOLVING

1. If you are doing this alone, choose the types of excursions that fit your personal thinking style best. Those exercises are most likely to be fun to play and therefore most likely to produce the desired ideas.

2. The more thoroughly you complete an excursion the more productive it will be. Resist the temptation to fly through excursions.

3. If you want to use the more fantasy-driven techniques, ask one or two close friends or confidantes to help you by playing the role of the other(s) in the group technique.

TIPS FOR BUSINESS PROBLEM SOLVING

1. If you are leading a group, plan twice as many excursions as you think you will need. This will provide you the

flexibility to change things up when energy in the group runs low, or to shift to techniques that better fit the thinking styles of your participants.

2. Plan techniques that are only a little bit uncomfortable for your team. If you're working with engineers or physicians who revel in data to find their ideas, don't make people close their eyes in the meeting room or throw a ball to the next participant as a means of calling on them. Instead, consider giving them LEGOs® or another moderate stretch technique that will feel a bit out of the ordinary but not embarrassing or uncomfortable to do.

3. Gather all your supplies in advance so you have them on hand when you need them. Take inventory of craft supplies, cards and other tools prior to your session, and have everything organized and ready to use in the moment.

CHAPTER ELEVEN

CONVERGING: SETTING STRATEGIC CRITERIA

Now that we have dozens and dozens of ideas to consider, it's time to begin the evaluation phase. This is the "convergence" portion of the CPS process, and the objective is to identify the lead ideas so the individual or group can continue to develop them.

It's important to apply some type of criteria to your selection process. Criteria can be as simple as your favorite ideas; more often than not, however, there are key business criteria that must be met before an idea can see the light of day.

Here's the tricky part: In a business setting, criteria can crush every single idea if you're not careful.

We will begin our discussion with what NOT to do.

WRONG: PROFITABILITY AND FEASIBILITY

As business people, we want to go immediately to our top criteria—"highly profitable" and "easily feasible"—when evaluating any idea.

While profitability and feasibility are critical to any business success, our criteria question centers on WHEN we apply it. When we're still working with phrases and simple sentences, it's too easy to dismiss—with a wave of the hand—a brilliant but roughly-articulated fledgling idea.

Applying profitability and feasibility criteria too early is a huge mistake for several reasons:

- An idea that is still a one-line statement has the potential to be developed in an infinite number of ways—some could prove to be "profitable" and "feasible," while others could be losing propositions. We simply don't yet have enough information to make a call on either set of criteria.

- At this point in the process, no one in the room could possibly predict profitability because of the large number of additional factors that ultimately affect profitability, including: cost of goods, cost of packaging material and labor, speed of production, quality assurance testing requirements, overhead, cost of advertising, etc. With all that information still unknown, guessing on profitability and feasibility would be premature.

- Some members of the group may have knowledge that could influence a decision prematurely. For example, the R&D team may have knowledge of emerging technologies that marketing managers are unaware of. Without this knowledge the total group led by marketing may decide too quickly that a high potential idea is unfeasible, when in reality it might be possible now. Many great ideas have been flushed down the toilet in this way. Regardless of managements' opinion of an idea, if it's tested with customers and proves to rock their world and become a necessity in their lives, I guarantee the company *will* find a way to make it profitably—with co-packers, fast-tracked internal development, a partnership with a non-competitor, or any one of many other options.

Instead of focusing on feasibility and profitability right away, we ask you to start with higher-level criteria and apply Greenhouse Thinking™. Taking those steps first will enable you to identify and communicate what's good about the idea to your customers, your consumers and your company. If it turns out to be a great idea from the consumer/customer viewpoint, you can move on to what you wish for in order to build on the idea, add to it, change it or build more like it.

RIGHT: ROUND ONE CRITERIA – HIGH-LEVEL STRATEGIC CRITERIA

Now we will discuss what you SHOULD do. When setting criteria, your objective is to provide a benchmark for identifying ideas with the highest potential. Your *first cut* must be done at a high level, to get your list down from several hundred to about 25 strong ideas. Your second or third cut can contain profitability and feasibility; we will address this in Chapter Twelve.

Begin by leading a high-level team discussion on strategic criteria that apply right now. The discussion itself creates a mindset to aid your "gut" as you ask yourself, "Is this a big idea?" As the group selects criteria, think about the needs of both your company and your end customer. Criteria might include:

1. Meets a true customer need and solves a problem for them
2. Unique in the marketplace; not a "me too" product
3. Broad appeal among our target audience
4. Fits with the values and equities of our brand
5. Your judgment that "This is a big idea!"

Sometimes additional guidelines can be applied, like, "Vote for a blend of short-term, medium-term and long-term ideas, to ensure we have an adequate innovation pipeline over the next five years" or "Emphasize short-term ideas but vote for at least 10% new-to-the-world options, so we have plenty of ideas to execute for next year and a few beyond that."

Let's discuss the criteria and why each one is important:

1. **Meets a true customer need, solves a problem for them** - Including this criterion ensures that you focus first and foremost on the end purchaser of the product or service. We cannot be successful if our customers believe our product is unnecessary. Conversely, we will be highly successful if we make our customers' lives better in a real way.

2. **Is unique in the marketplace, not a "me too" product** - Many companies are looking to truly innovate, not just copy the competition's success. If they are going to invest in innovation, they want to ensure success by entering the market with an offering difficult to replicate that will delay or discourage competition from copying the idea. This provides a sustainable competitive advantage that allows the investment to pay for itself over time.

3. **Has broad appeal within our target market** - When businesses consider the significant investment that innovation requires, they try to ensure they will receive adequate volume from any new product or service, and that the volume will be sustainable over time. Years ago, when most marketers sold to the "mass market" (ages 18-55), no one wanted to invent a "niche" product with limited appeal. Now, as we are increasingly able to target one individual at a time through social media and other techniques, niche products are much more attractive, as long as the niche is considered "deep"—which means it has a lot of potential repeat business within it, even if the audience size is small.

4. **Fits with the values and equities of our brand** - Every company must consider this criterion carefully for a couple of reasons.

First of all, consumers give us "permission" to go only so far with our brands before new products or services feel like a mismatch to them. An example of this is the Car Repair and Chocolate Shop. For customers of a car repair company, many things will make sense as potential areas of expansion: selling tires, tools for do-it-yourself car repair buffs, auto accessories, even driver's training could fit. But once you throw in the Chocolate Shop, people begin to say, "Whaaaaa????"

Secondly, companies spend millions every year to protect their reputations. A company such as Nickelodeon would never want to build neighborhood bars and pubs; they simply don't fit with the brand's values. And while a company like Twitter would probably never introduce after-school snacks for teens, it may want to target teens by creating teen forums, closed friendship tween groups, tween contests, even hip t-shirts or phone cases that might appeal to teens.

5. **Earns your judgment that "This is a big idea!"** - Many client teams resist this criterion because it's too "squishy" or "fuzzy" to be real. However, I usually advocate for them to include it, because reading 768 ideas in two hours and lining each one up to each criterion before deciding is not practical. In reality, people are able to keep the criteria discussion in the back of their minds as they read each idea and ask, "Yes, or no? Is this a big idea?"

Setting the right criteria at the right time—and more importantly, putting every team member on a level playing field in the selection process—is key to success in convergence.

SUMMARY OF CHAPTER ELEVEN – CONVERGING: SETTING EVALUATION CRITERIA

1. The purpose of setting strategic criteria is to provide a mindset to aid your "gut judgments" in evaluating hundreds of ideas at a time.

2. Do not consider profitability or feasibility in the first cut of evaluation criteria. They belong in Criteria Round #2 or #3.

3. Instead, consider high-level criteria that are relevant to both the end customer purchasing the innovation, and to you as a business entity.

4. Recommended First Cut criteria include:
    - Meets a true customer need and solves a problem for them
    - Is unique in the marketplace and not a "me too" product
    - Has broad appeal within our target audience(s)
    - Fits with the values and equities of our brand
    - Group judgment is, "This is a big idea!"

5. Allow consumer testing to winnow your list down to the best ideas before looking at feasibility and profitability. If an idea scores big, companies somehow find a way to make it profitable and feasible.

TIPS FOR PERSONAL PROBLEM SOLVING

1. Your criteria need to be modified to address a personal problem; as such, they might include:
    - Meets my needs, accomplishes what I intended
    - Truly solves my problem

- Represents something I can get excited about taking on as a challenge
- Fits with my values and the way I live my life
- My judgment is, "This feels like a great idea!"

2. Do not think about the cost of each solution YET. Assume you can make anything free or affordable, and focus on the idea itself and its ability to solve your problem.

3. Resist temptation to eliminate ideas that seem difficult or complicated. Again, assume every idea is somehow doable. Then, the ideas that rise to the top are there for you to work with and make feasible.

TIPS FOR BUSINESS PROBLEM SOLVING

1. Allow your group to discuss criteria and discover them on their own. You can open up the discussion by posing the question, "What needs to be true of an idea in order for you to move it forward?" This will help the team feel ownership with the criteria, which will make the next steps easier.

2. As your team suggests criteria, jot them down and clarify each one to ensure the whole group understands and agrees. For example, "uniqueness" is a subjective idea. Does the team want to be unique in the world? In the nation? In the region? In the category? Or is some element of "me too" okay as long as we build a better mousetrap when we move to execution? You must clarify your team's definitions of each criterion and make sure everyone understands it the same way.

3. If someone from your team mentions profitability or feasibility, write the word down on a separate flip chart page entitled, "Second Cut Criteria" and explain why you are putting it there. That will make participants feel heard, and confident that their comment was valued instead of dismissed. Announce to the group that additional criteria will be added to the second cut after idea development.

CHAPTER TWELVE

CONVERGING: APPLYING VISION AND SELECTING THE LEAD IDEAS

Now that we have developed our strategic criteria, it's time to select our lead ideas.

ADOPTING THE RIGHT MINDSET FOR EVALUATION

At this point the tendency to "Yes, but . . ." can hit full force. A "Yes, but . . ." response comes in many forms and can negate good work and ideas. For example:

- Putting all the ideas into a report without converging is the same thing as tossing away every idea. None will ever see the light of day, and we have wasted a whole lot of time and resources creating the ideas in the first place.

- Having your internal employees evaluate the ideas can also be a source of "Yes, but . . ." responses because they tend to be incredibly biased and may not view the ideas the same way customers would. They also can't help but think of themselves and how each idea would affect their personal work load.

- And, the "shove it down their throats" approach that sometimes happens when one top manager decides for everyone, usually chips away at team relationships and commitment to the project.

"Yes, but . .." examples abound throughout history. Below are a few of my favorite quotes:

- During a 1927 discussion of a new idea to replace silent movies with "talkies," H.M. Warner of Warner Brothers said, "Who the hell wants to hear actors talk?"

- When being recruited to work in oil fields, workers in 1859 said to Edwin L. Drake, "You mean drill in the ground to try to find oil?! You're crazy."

- In 1895, Albert Einstein's teacher told Albert's father that, "It doesn't matter what he does. He will never amount to anything."

- When the President of the Michigan Savings Bank refused to invest in Ford Motor Company, he said, "The horse is here to stay, but the automobile is only a novelty, a fad."

- Just yesterday your boss said to your colleague, "Forget it. That idea costs too much." I wonder what brilliant innovation got squashed that time.

All these quotes have one thing in common — a complete lack of VISION. Every time we immerse ourselves in a "Yes, but . . .." we close our eyes to a possible better future.

But this is a Catch 22. We limit ourselves because, as business managers, we don't have permission to fail. We MUST succeed, or we will find ourselves escorted out of the office for the last time with a box of personal items in hand. The message we get is that in a competitive world, we must never make a mistake because everyone—and I mean everyone-- is instantly replaceable.

And because we must not fail, it's much more prudent to suggest a small, workable idea when recommending a course of action, because we know everyone is likely to agree, and the idea won't ruffle any feathers in the process. But small ideas can only take us so far. This anecdote about Marvel Comics is the perfect illustration:

> In the 1930s, comic books became a popular means of escape from the real world, which, at the time, was mired in a world war. Because they made us feel powerful against our enemies, the popularity of comic books soared. When they were first published, Marvel Comics' Avengers comic books were sold for twelve cents. Each month, the publishers made a few more dimes, and a few more the following month, and so on and so forth.
>
> A company with limited vision could carry on this way for quite some time.
>
> Because they were so fun and engaging, many companies eyed the Marvel franchise for business possibilities. Without vision, it's easy to look at the business and say, "Why would I want to buy a comic book company that only makes 12 cents a sale? There are much better revenue opportunities out there. I'll pass."
>
> However, by the 1970s and beyond, visionary business people began to see the opportunities. Why not build other products and entertainments from the success of the comic

books? Why not create a superhero live-action TV show? Superhero cartoons? Licensed lunchboxes? Halloween costumes? Licensed backpacks? Action figures? Mugs? T-shirts? Blockbuster movies? The list is unlimited, and that's the reason Marvel Comics is the powerhouse brand we know today, despite its humble beginnings.

How do we apply vision? Simply use Greenhouse Thinking™. Ask yourself, what do I like about the idea? What do I wish for to solve any concerns I have about the idea? Then, once you note the answer to each of these questions explicitly, push further and ask, "How can I make this a HUGE idea?" It's amazing what we can see in an idea when we approach it with a larger vision.

IDEA SELECTION PROCESSES

Business people have all kinds of ideas about the "best" way to select ideas, including many I'd put into the "seat of the pants" category. I've heard comments like:

- "I already decided on the one idea I heard that I liked."
- "We give the idea list to R&D and they throw them all out except for the few they think they can do."
- "We give them all to our Legal Department and they kill all of the ideas, except maybe one or, if we're lucky, two or three."
- "Our manager is an egomaniac so he will make the choice, and we'll all suck it up and execute."

Yikes! That's a lot of negativity!

Selection processes that are not helpful:

<u>Grouping Ideas</u>

Another favorite approach among business people when evaluating many ideas is to try to "group" or "bucket" them by similarities before voting. When this method is used, we end up with only a handful of things (buckets) to vote on and can easily choose the best option within the grouping, right?

WRONG. Grouping or bucketing is the worst thing you can do to a group of ideas, because it:

- Wipes out the uniqueness within each idea, which leaves only high-level, generalized clichés that every one of your competitors has already considered.

- Takes each idea at face value instead of allowing the team to apply VISION to each idea, to ensure it lives up to its potential.

- Forces you to touch every single idea whether it's useful or not, which is a BIG waste of time. Why not just touch the best ones and leave the rest behind?

<u>Ranking Ideas in Order of Your Interest</u>

Another favorite approach among business people is to have individuals prioritize all the ideas, making the best idea #1, the next best #2 and so on, all the way down to #789 — the "worst" idea. This will clearly identify the winning ideas, right?

WRONG. Prioritizing ideas individually is a nightmare because it:

- Takes a very long time for each person to complete, so it's very inefficient.

- Requires the ranker to make judgments on ideas with only infinitesimal differences. So, for example, is the idea that I ranked #677 really a little bit better than the idea I ranked as #678? Delineations this small are simply not meaningful.

- Is impossible to gather results from the entire team without using a complex algorithm that weights each idea.

Selection processes that *are* helpful:

Vote Yes or No

Instead of asking individuals to group or prioritize, we recommend VOTING "yes" or "pass" (meaning no) for each idea. Here is how it works: Read the idea and ask yourself, "Does this fit the criteria we just discussed? Yes or no?" Alternatively, you can ask, "Is this a big idea? Yes or no?"

Using our CyberGreenhouse™ Online Co-Creation tool, our clients simply click on the "thumbs up" button next to ideas they like and skip over ideas they don't. The system instantly uses the team's collective votes to rank ideas according to team interest.

Here is a fictional example of a new product co-creation for the US Postal Service that focuses on new stamp ideas. Sample criteria are on the right.

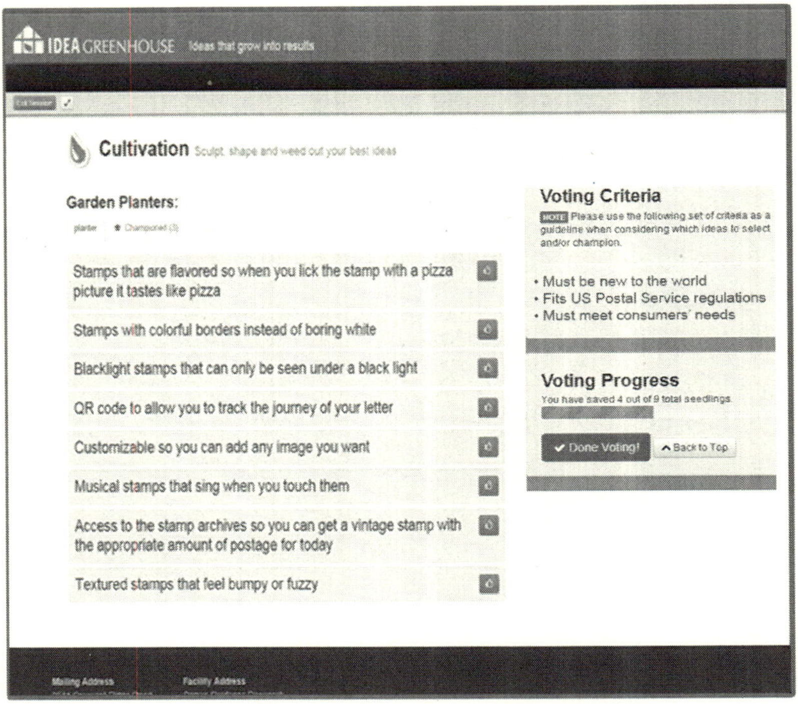
IDEA GREENHOUSE
Ideas that grow into results
Cultivation
Sculpt, shape and weed out your best ideas
Garden Planters:
Stamps that are flavored so when you lick the stamp with a pizza picture it tastes like pizza
Stamps with colorful borders instead of boring white
Blacklight stamps that can only be seen under a black light
QR code to allow you to track the journey of your letter
Customizable so you can add any image you want
Musical stamps that sing when you touch them
Access to the stamp archives so you can get a vintage stamp with the appropriate amount of postage for today
Textured stamps that feel bumpy or fuzzy
Voting Criteria
NOTE Please use the following set of criteria as a guideline when considering which ideas to select and/or champion.
• Must be new to the world
• Fits US Postal Service regulations
• Must meet consumers' needs
Voting Progress
You have saved 4 out of 9 total seedlings
Done Voting!
Back to Top
Mailing Address
Facility Address

If you don't have access to an online voting tool, you can still easily capture team votes by using the low-tech system that worked for decades before our electronic system was invented and built. Start by making a paper copy of all ideas for each team member, trying not to think about the trees being killed in the process.

Then follow these instructions:

1. Ask the group to vote for up to **?** number of different ideas by making a small x in the left margin next to the bullet point.

   You determine the number of votes each team member gets by dividing the total number of ideas by 3. For example, if you had 789 ideas listed, each team member should vote for up to approximately 260. This number does not need to be precise; it is chosen strictly to ensure that a team of about eight to ten people can converge on a group of almost 800 ideas.

If you make the mistake of assigning too few votes, you will not get enough overlap on any single idea to allow it to rise to the top. If you assign too many votes, you'll never make a mistake, because there will always be plenty of overlap, and it will be easy to see where the team's interest lies. The only downside of asking for too many votes is that the team may not find that many ideas they truly like and will be forced to vote for some that they're not enamored with.

Typically, four or five votes per typed page is perfect. Tell the team, "If you've made it through several pages and voted for nothing, loosen up! By the same token, if you find yourself voting for eight or nine ideas per page, tighten up! Your target of 260 is a rough guideline."

2. Remove Order Bias.

    Ask 1/3 of the room to start at the front of the deck and work toward the back. Ask another 1/3 of the room to start at the last page and read backwards to the front. The final 1/3 should "cut the cards" somewhere in the middle and work front to back. This eliminates order bias due to the fatigue that invariably sets in at some point, so the last ideas you read somehow never receive the scrutiny you gave to the first few ideas.

3. Keep voting guidelines in mind:

- Identify the "likes" and keep them alive by bringing them to the top of the list.

- Don't be too literal—if you like most of the idea but don't care for a few details, vote for it anyway, knowing you can modify the idea with Greenhouse Thinking before moving it forward.

- Work alone—after all the ideas are ranked, you will have an opportunity to work together to discuss and develop each one. For this step, you need many distinct perspectives, which individual judgment will deliver, so it's important to work alone at this step.

4. Vote for all duplicates of the ideas you LIKE. Invariably, within a large list of ideas there will be some overlap. And since brains don't think in neat little buckets, topics can run together, and by late afternoon it's easy to forget ideas that were mentioned first thing in the morning.

    - Here is your instruction: "If you see an idea you LIKE, vote for it every time you see it, even if there is some minor variation among them. We do it this way because if one person votes for the idea only on page 3 and another person votes for it only on page 24 and a third person votes for it only on page 70, it will appear that only one person liked the idea. In reality three did, but we missed those other votes. Remember, you are voting for up to 260 *different* ideas, so every duplicate counts as the same idea; because of this, don't be concerned if you end up with 280 votes or more."

    - Make sure to emphasize that in the final ranking you will skip over an idea the second time it appears, and consider it done. In this way, all duplicates will be eliminated.

- "Finally, take risks! It is so easy to vote for only easy, safe, mainstream ideas. But don't be tempted—your competitors have already thought of these ideas, as did management, years ago. True innovation can make you a little bit uncomfortable, especially if you are looking to build a long-term pipeline of innovations to introduce over the next several years. Push yourself to vote for at least 26 ideas (10%) that make you a bit uncomfortable, ideas your gut tells you would be huge if you pulled them off!"

- This is a silent activity. Do not allow chatting phone calls or breaks, which disrupts other voters and delays the whole team, because all team members must finish voting before tallies can be made.

5. As your team is silently reading and voting on their own printouts, tape each page of the master copy to the wall in page order.

6. Ask participants to transfer their votes from their own paper to the master deck on the wall after they finish voting. Everyone should move in the same direction (front of deck to back of deck) as they transfer their votes, although you may decide to start them on different pages to avoid traffic jams at the walls.

7. After all votes have been transferred, you will need to walk along the wall and underline all ideas that received votes from more than half of your team. Those are your "winning ideas!" If your objective was to find six big ideas, take the

top six. If your objective was to generate 25 new ideas, keep going down the list of votes until you have 25.

Champion Ideas

This is a wonderful technique to balance out your voting evaluation process. Still using the strategic criteria set by the team, ask participants to finish voting and then select ONE idea within the list of 789 that they, personally, feel passionately about pursuing, regardless of how the votes fall.

Sometimes we ask for a "favorite" idea, to ensure the top passion ideas make it into the mix regardless of team votes. With other groups we ask for a "stretch" idea, to ensure we wind up with a rich, robust pipeline of ideas. You choose, based on your objectives and strategic needs.

The reason we use this technique is that it leads to the optimal blend of ideas. Ideas selected by team vote are likely to be extremely broad, mainstream and safe, given the fact that your whole diverse team agrees on them. By identifying the "passion" ideas, we are able to include truly new and different options that have the potential to bring about big growth or create whole new categories, even though they may be a bit riskier.

In the end, this dual process yields an ideal blend of ideas and a range of risk profiles, so management can pursue innovation efforts that fit their appetite for risk.

Rate Ideas

As we mentioned in Chapter Eight on "Territory," rating is a great technique to use when you have a maximum of 20 ideas—a very short list.

Keep in mind that rating is NOT Ranking, a technique that puts ideas in a sequence according to appeal. *Rating* means assigning a number to every idea on this list, on a scale from 0-5, where 0 = I hate this idea and 5 = I adore this idea. Participants can give all 0s, all 5s or anything in between.

SUMMARY OF CHAPTER TWELVE – CONVERGENCE: SELECTING THE LEAD IDEAS

1. Always start with a positive mindset.

2. Apply VISION and focus on the potential in an idea, not the idea at face value.

3. Give clear instructions and vote "yes" or "no" on each idea.

4. Select ONE passion idea to champion as a favorite or stretch idea.

5. If your idea list is <20, rate all your ideas from 0-5; you can review this process in Chapter Eight.

TIPS FOR PERSONAL PROBLEM SOLVING

1. If you are working alone, you are likely to have a shorter list. Use the rating system instead of the voting system to identify your best ideas.

2. Consider crafting your criteria in a different way if you choose to rate your ideas. In this case, craft your criteria to focus on *degrees* of fit, such as how comprehensive the solution is, how well you can integrate this into your life, how long-term the solution is, etc. That will allow you to address each criterion with a numerical rating that answers the question, "To what *degree* does this idea fits my criteria?"

3. Select fewer options as your "lead ideas" if you are working alone, since the next step of idea development is likely to be more complicated.

TIPS FOR BUSINESS PROBLEM SOLVING

1. Allow at least two hours for voting if you do not have voting technology; some people read more slowly than others, and some weigh their options longer than others who make faster judgments.

2. Take time to emphasize the idea of applying vision. You will have a much stronger end list of top ideas if you do. If time permits, have the team do some sample exercises to practice first, such as passing out children's' toys and posing the question to your team, "how could you make this a huge idea?"

3. If you are working with a team for whom English is a second language, add at least 50% more time to your session, as these team members need more time to work through the additional cognitive step of translating each idea before making a judgment.

4. Be tough on squelching chit-chat during voting, as it will make voting take longer and cause your meeting to run late. If that happens, people will try to exit the meeting before it's over and leave you hanging; or they will stay late, perhaps be late for child care pick-up and be angry that the session is taking so long. One easy way to do this is to sit silently in the room while people are voting; you feel like a "teacher" to them and they instantly focus on their task without you needing to say a single word.

5. Always end this session with a list of top ideas. Seeing them all written clearly and neatly in one place will be a great reward or "payoff" for the group, and help them feel they've accomplished something important. Which they have!

CHAPTER THIRTEEN

DEVELOPING THE LEAD IDEAS

Now that we've identified our lead ideas through a combination of voting and champion techniques, it's time to expand them into fully developed options.

I say "options" because we still want a range of ideas to consider, so we can ask our consumers or customers to decide which ideas appeal to them the most. Best practices dictate that we develop several ideas to about "80% perfect" and then let our customers react, build on and optimize them to add the last 20%. This approach frees management from selecting one best idea, creating a risk that customers might not agree with the choice.

Multiple solutions can also create the potential for a longer-term pipeline that prepares the business for today, next year and 5-10 years down the road.

To develop this range of ideas, we build the high-interest snippets or one-line ideas into fully thought-through, well-communicated concepts or plans. Technically we are diverging again, because we are expanding instead of contracting our options; but this expansion is limited to fleshing out an idea in more detail—with just enough information so that consumers or customers understand it well enough to evaluate it, and others involved in implementation can understand it as well.

There are several different ways to define an idea depending on what you're trying to accomplish.

IDEA FORMATS FOR CONSUMER TESTING

Most companies test their lead ideas with their customers or consumers before investing additional time and money in figuring out feasibility, profitability, legalities, etc. The reason? If an idea proves to be essential to every household in America, chances are very high that a company will figure out a way to solve all the other challenges. Conversely, if an idea is highly unappealing to customers or consumers, there is no reason to waste any time or money addressing the related challenges.

Several different formats have proven effective when testing ideas with customers or consumers. We will outline each below, and explain when and how to use each format.

1. Problem-Solution-Benefit

While this is not the most popular format, starting our description with the problem-solution-benefit format makes the other options easier to understand.

Problem: This is the difficulty facing a consumer or customer for which a solution is required. For obvious reasons, this often shows up as a negative statement such as, "I get so dirty fixing my car that it's impossible to get my hands completely clean."

Solution: This is the company product or service that addresses the difficulty. It should be a direct answer to the problem stated above. An example of a solution might be "Deep Scrub Paste for Men is a new pumice formula from the makers of GOOP Hand Cleaner."

Benefit: This answers the question, "What do I GET from this product?" and solves the original problem. In this example, the benefit is "gets your hands completely clean in seconds."

Here is how it would look in a concept:

Introducing **New Deep Scrub Paste for Men**

For complete clean in seconds

Weekend warriors get so greasy fixing cars that it seems impossible to get hands and nails completely clean.

New Deep Scrub Paste for Men is a new pumice formula from the makers of GOOP.

It gets even the greasiest hands and nails completely clean in seconds, without skin irritation.

When to use this format: Use this for business problem solving when your team is made up of less sophisticated marketers. Problem statements are more straightforward, and also easier to understand and create when compared to the options listed below.

Disadvantages of this format: No one likes reading about upsetting problems, guilt, pain, irritation or other negatives. In fact, starting on a note that's too negative can create a "big hole" to climb out of and require a miracle solution to turn things around.

Sometimes the negative statement is such a turn-off that consumers don't hear anything beyond the first statement—they get "stuck in the yuck." If you choose this format, make sure your problems are not expressed too negatively.

2. Insight-Benefit-Reason to Believe

This has been the most popular format among businesses for many years, perhaps because when P&G adopted it early on, it became the testing gold standard for the consumer packaged goods industry.

Insight: Similar to the "problem" listed above, this is defined as an essential consumer truth or deeply-held consumer belief that governs the way consumers see a *situation*—before a product or service is introduced. Always expressed in the first person, this can also be thought of as the "premise." It is often a positive statement of beliefs or values, and sometimes contains a point of tension or an unmet consumer need. But the statement is always more positive than negative.

This is a popular format because, as we saw above, a positive first statement has a big effect on how positively consumers respond to an idea.

For example, compare these two statements:

(Problem Set-Up)

I frequently get migraines, and when they come on the pain just pounds and pounds and pounds, and once it takes hold, it takes a fistful of medicine to get relief.

(Insight Set-Up)

I suffer from migraines from time to time, and it's important for me to get ahead of the pain when I feel one coming on.

The first statement in and of itself gives me a headache! The second one still paints a clear picture but isn't so negative that I am unable to move on to the solution.

Other examples of insights for migraine medication might include:

Migraines can really interrupt my day, so I always want to be prepared.

I have a busy, full life and don't want to slow down for anything, especially a migraine.

Migraines can get in the way of getting things done, and slowing down is not an option for me.

I'm more likely to get a migraine when there is noise and chaos around me, but I can't always control my environment completely.

See how different these positive statements are from the "problem" statements above?

Benefit:

Just as in the Problem-Solution-Benefit format listed above, this answers the question, "What do I get" from your solution / product / service?" It should be a direct response to the Insight above, but it should not communicate product attributes like, "It is fast acting." The benefit in this format is about me, me and me, the customer or consumer ("I get fast relief").

Reason to Believe:

These are "facts" about the product or service that prove the benefit will be delivered. The word "facts" appears in quotes because it can be a true fact—something about a unique ingredient or a proprietary production process—or a perceived fact, like, "It's the favorite choice of pro athletes." Another popular term for reason to believe is "support."

If we are trying to support the idea of "I get fast relief," examples of reasons to believe include:

- It has a new, fast-acting formula that relieves pain in as little as 20 minutes.
- It has a new micro-thin coating that is easy on your stomach and dissolves quickly so it goes to work right away.
- It has a new formula based on natural products research so your body absorbs it quickly.
- It's the number one choice for doctors and nurses who can't afford to let a migraine ruin their day.

Here is how it would look in a concept:

> *Introducing* **New Migrainia from Bayer**
>
> *The fast way to beat a migraine*
>
> Migraines can get in the way of getting things done, and slowing down is not an option for me.
>
> New Migrainia from Bayer gives me the fastest relief available for my migraines.
>
> That's because its new fast-acting formula dissolves and enters my blood stream within seconds, so it works faster than any other brand.

When to use this format: Use this whenever you are going to consumer testing, either qualitative or quantitative. I prefer writing in the first person because consumers seem to accept statements more readily when the language reflects an individual expressing an opinion; consumers are less accepting of statements that tell them how they feel.

Disadvantages of this format: If you select the wrong insight, your concept will be disliked regardless of what else it says. Check your insight statement and ask yourself, "Would everyone in this consumer group agree with this statement?" If your answer is "no," rewrite it so that it reflects a universally accepted belief.

3. Description – Benefit

This format is simpler than the two listed above. Use it when you are working on personal problem solving, because the problem itself is already imbedded in your consciousness. This also works well in business problem solving when the problem is very simple but the solution is complex. For example, if you're targeting college students learning to manage their money, it's not necessary to mention money management as the problem in every concept. By the same token, the description of the solution is likely to be complex because it addresses many different elements of financial planning.

Description: This is a short blurb about your product, service or action that describes what it is and what it does. Give it enough detail to describe all aspects of the plan, but not so much that you lose the reader. I find that a short description with a list of bullet-pointed features works well.

Benefits: This is just like the "I get" statements mentioned above. Be sure to focus on what the user gets, not what the product/service is.

Examples of benefits for a college student's money management plan may include:

- I get a clear path to follow so I'll always know what to do next to reach my goals.
- I get a feeling of security about my future.
- I get a gauge to measure myself against, so I always know where I am on the path to my goals.
- I get a clearly defined strategic "touchstone" that makes all my financial decisions easy, because they are grounded in my values.
- I get a guaranteed sunny financial future.
- I get additional knowledge from practicing my plan which gives me confidence and will help me improve continuously over time.

Here is how it would look in a concept:

> **New Youth Banking from Bank of America**
>
> *The fast way to a strong financial future*
>
> New Youth Banking from Bank of America is a unique service designed for those who are new to financial planning and budgeting, and want to build their skills. It includes:
>
> - Your own homepage with a dashboard showing where you are with all accounts
> - Overdraft warnings by text, with time to remedy the situation
> - Overdraft coverage up to $50 per month
> - A fun budgeting tool that maps your "journey" to financial independence
> - Tips for minimizing interest, consolidating debt, and savings plans
> - Online chat 24/7 with your personal youth banker to answer any questions
> - Bonus rewards of $10 per month that you avoid overdraft
>
> It gives me the fastest path possible to my financial freedom.

When to use this format: This works great when the situation is simple and the product or service itself is fairly complex, has multiple features and needs a longer explanation. Use this for banking services, insurance products, software, etc.

Disadvantages of this format: This format does not allow you to include an insight or problem to be solved, so it must be implied. When you need to communicate multiple features, something will have to go, as consumers will lose interest if you ask them to digest too much information at once.

4. Visual Concepts

As American consumers become accustomed to communication that is visual instead of verbal, some companies are choosing to eliminate words altogether, and instead showing consumers a photo-shopped image, a photo or physical prototype, video, or other visuals for consumers to evaluate.

This is great for new product "gizmos" that have a physical form. Here is a great example of a visual concept for a solar phone charger from a tech project several years ago (when solar chargers were a brand new idea!)

Visual concepts do *not* work well for testing the communication messages underlying an advertisement, because there are— obviously-- no words on visual concepts.

Two important cautions when using visual concepts:

1. If you are showing consumers a new food or beverage idea, pay close attention to appetite appeal! If it doesn't look totally yummy in your visual, people will hate the idea even if the product itself is highly appealing.

2. When you use a visual concept, strive to ONLY depict the new idea. Do not be tempted to provide background, environmental context, place settings, "moods" or any other

extraneous information. This anecdote illustrates the reason perfectly.

> A few years ago I conducted a project for a major makeup manufacturer who wanted to develop a new line of makeup for young women. The client insisted on visual concepts that represented the "mood" of the product line but did not want to ever show the product itself. The resulting concepts were "lifestyle mood boards"–collages essentially--that the clients thought captured the image and mood of this new makeup line.
>
> Given the fact that all makeup and perfume are about fantasy and how they make a woman feel, this didn't seem like a crazy request. As a result we complied with our clients' decision and made visual "mood" concept collages. As soon as they were completed and approved, we took them to qualitative testing with representative consumers.
>
> The qualitative groups were a complete and total disaster! We could not get the women to comment on the product itself or the way it makes them feel, and whether or not they thought it was a good idea. Instead we heard respondents say things like,
>
> - "That tablecloth is not my taste, so I would never buy this product."
> - "The guy on that motorcycle isn't very cute so I would never look twice at this product."
> - "I think collages are disorganized, so I think this product would be confusing if I saw it on the shelf."

Not a single respondent could even imagine the product line itself, so we learned a lot about extraneous images and *nothing* about the product appeal. Our mistake was creating visuals that were too metaphorical for consumers to respond to.

When to use this format: This works very well for physical new products when the visual is clear and speaks for itself. It also works well for concepts targeted to kids or non-English speaking target audiences, since it requires no reading. You can add a title as the only verbal communication to set context, and read the title to the respondents.

Disadvantages of this format: When consumers see visuals, they take them *literally*, and have a difficult time thinking of the product as an idea that can be built on and changed. In addition, the image must be thought-through completely from all angles, checking carefully that you have removed all the extraneous imagery of any kind that could cloud the idea. This will ensure you get a clean read on what is driving the appeal of the idea.

5. Action Plans

I love this format because it takes a very thorough look at what needs to be done, which makes it that much easier to actually get it done. I refer to the elements I like to use for this as the 5 Ws: who, what, when, where, why and, of course, one H: how.

By way of explanation, let's imagine we just completed a brainstorm session on the fictional topic, "How to increase Millennial store traffic at JC Penney." Let's imagine one lead idea is stated as follows: "Create highly targeted weekly email deals to bring Millennials into the store." Here is the example:

WHO: Marketing Communications department, led by Jane Jones

WHAT: Targeted weekly email deals sent to Millennials to bring them into the store.

WHEN: Every week, on Tuesday mornings at 2am

WHERE: Direct email, Facebook messages, Instagram messages, Blogs, Groupon, other social media TBD

WHY: Millennials see us as "grandma's store", and we need to refresh our image to remain relevant. Our average shopper is a 52 year old, white woman who lives in suburban areas. We must become popular with younger shoppers if we are to sustain our business over the next 20 years.

Past research says that the Millennials' average trip into the store is triggered by needing one item; if we can trigger that trip via email, we will reap 3 times the revenue, because once Millennials are in the store, they buy on average 3.6 items, increasing our transaction ring by about $43 vs. what they came in for.

Electronic communication will update our "stodgy" image among Millennials.

HOW: Marketing Communications works with Operations, Regional Store Managers, and a social media consultant to be determined, to gather emails and begin tracking activity.

Design an algorithm ala Amazon to suggest purchases based on history, and to design motivating offers.

Work with agency to create a word-of-mouth program as an overlay to social media

Program complete and in market no later than January 31, 2018

Resources required (as you fill out this section, think: Time? Money? Human resources?)

- o Budget of $X
- o 10 hours a week x 5 weeks Operations representative
- o 5 hours a week x 5 weeks Marketing representative
- o 20 hours a week x 5 weeks Social Media consultant
- o Oversight by division manager 1 hour week x 5 weeks

When to use this format: This is great to use for business or personal problem solving, when you don't plan to do customer or consumer testing and you need an internal document with clear "marching orders" for next steps.

Disadvantages of this format: This is not a good format for any consumer testing. It's too detailed and is designed for an internal team, not an external audience.

To summarize, this step builds your one-line snippets into fully thought-through, well-communicated concepts or plans. Remember to include just enough information in your final concepts so consumers understand it well enough to evaluate it, and others involved in implementation can understand it. Make sure you haven't added too much detail, because that can create confusion.

SUMMARY OF CHAPTER THIRTEEN – DEVELOPING THE LEAD IDEAS

1. Once you have identified your lead one-line ideas through the voting and championing processes, the next step is to develop them into a range of clear concepts. The trick is to elaborate on each lead idea just enough to allow you to accurately evaluate its appeal and market potential, but not so much that readers get information overload.

2. Several formats work well for this step; select the one best for your purposes.
   - Problem-Solution-Benefit
   - Insight-Benefit-Reason to Believe
   - Description-Benefit
   - Visual Concepts
   - Action Plan: who, what, when, where, why, how

3. Once your concepts or plans are developed, it's time to apply Cut #2 and Cut #3 of Criteria; this will be discussed in the next chapter.

TIPS FOR PERSONAL PROBLEM SOLVING

1. If you are working alone, consider using either the Description-Benefit or Action Plan format, because they are more appropriate for more complex issues.

2. If you choose to create Action Plans, pay particular attention to the "why"—the closer "why" comes to your deep-seated values, the more successful you are likely to be.

3. In addition, if you choose to work with Action Plans, pay close attention to the "how" section, because that will provide your roadmap to success.

TIPS FOR BUSINESS PROBLEM SOLVING

1. If your next step is consumer testing of communication or a service, we strongly recommend using format #2: Insight-Benefit-Reason to Believe. The reason: Including the right insight can make a concept "sing." When we get the insight right, consumers conclude, "That company understands me."

2. If your next step is consumer testing of a physical new product, Visual Concepts work well but only if you do them right without extraneous visuals or metaphorical "mood" visuals. Give it a title as your only verbal communication.

3. If your next step is product development, an Action Plan will take you further with less effort. If you clearly outline the team's intentions, your internal resources can work more efficiently to reach your goal because there is less guesswork.

4. If you do an Action Plan, be sure to allow room for the Product Development team or other executing team members to apply their own expertise; clearly define the desired end result, but don't dictate too many details for how to achieve it, because that will create team frustration and underutilize your talent and resources.

CHAPTER FOURTEEN

QUALITY CHECK AND PRACTICAL CONSIDERATIONS: APPLYING CRITERIA #2 AND #3

Now that we have developed a range of ideas—either in concept format or action plan format—it is time to apply our second set of criteria, with tighter constraints than those we used to make the first cut.

As you recall from Chapter Eleven on Evaluation Criteria, we asked you to keep an open mind when you cut your ideas from several hundred down to about 25-35. That's because if we apply criteria here that are too limiting, we will not allow enough options to fall through the funnel, providing very little to work with. Twenty-five to thirty-five is still a big number, but it allows some imperfect ideas to fall through the funnel as well—so that later we can apply vision and Greenhouse Thinking™ to build them into strong, compelling, well-communicated concepts.

CRITERIA #2: CONCEPT COMMUNICATION CRITERIA

The criteria below can be applied to the range of ideas as a means of quality control:

- Is each idea truly breakthrough? (If not, adjust them.)
- Is each idea treated in a consistent way to ensure a fair shake in testing? (If not, make them all consistent.)
- Is each idea truly distinct from the others? (If not, rewrite to separate ideas.)
- Do we have a rich enough range of ideas? (If not, push yourself to add a couple of "riskier" ideas to the mix; if we don't have some bad ideas, we don't know where our limits are and therefore, we haven't stretched far enough!)
- Is each idea single-minded as written? (If not, rewrite so that each idea reflects only one offering with one benefit and one related RTB.)
- Are we testing short-term, medium-term and long-term innovation ideas? (If not, fill in additional ideas to ensure all three are represented)

Did you notice we are still leaving out profitability and feasibility?

We've done that because it's time for consumer testing, to determine the size of the prize, and provide management with clear direction on consumer priorities.

If you look at each concept/plan one at a time and can answer "yes" to each of the above questions, then we know we have a high quality set of ideas that are ready to be put in front of consumers. If taken to consumer or customer testing, we are likely to get meaningful results because:

- Each idea is testably different from the others—different enough for consumers to notice.
- Each idea has the same fair shot at winning.

Qualitative testing is helpful to do first, because you can get initial reactions to the ideas—including the "why" behind the appeal—in time to rewrite and optimize them before investing in a robust, volume-projection test, a test market that determines market potential, or a national roll-out.

Many consumer packaged goods companies today do not believe in quantitative testing because of the time and expense, and are even questioning how well these tests actually predict marketplace results. However, there is still a risk of throwing a seasonal product onto the shelves to try it out, or producing a unique product for one large retail customer to try before deciding to make it a permanent offering nationwide. All of these next steps are very expensive and carry significant financial risk, so it can be smart to spend just a little on qualitative testing like focus groups, to make sure you're leading with your best foot forward.

CRITERIA #3: FEASIBILITY AND PROFITABILITY—AFTER CONSUMER TEST RESULTS ARE IN

Following consumer or cutomer testing, you can turn over the winning optimized ideas with their results to Product Development, the agency, etc. for development and execution.

Finally—it's time to look at feasibility and profitability.

And NOW is the time because we are working with only one or two options—which we KNOW have strong market potential—instead of determining both of these things for ten possible ideas. When we dedicate our limited resources to developing these innovations, we know we are focusing on those projects with the greatest potential to grow our businesses and meet our strategic goals.

How to evaluate feasibility and profitability? For assessing feasibility, check with your friends in R&D and Operations, to help create realistic assumptions about raw materials, packaging materials, production line configurations, co-packer options and more. Based on other, similar products or services, a reasonable feasibility assessment can be made.

R&D and/or Operations can also help you create realistic assumptions for profitability, about: cost of goods, packaging costs, labor and production costs, equipment throughput speeds, marketing and distribution expenses, retail slotting allowances, company overhead, etc. You can also make an assessment based on products or services within your company that may have a similar cost structure.

One caution about assessing feasibility and profitability: it's important for your internal experts to continue to use Greenhouse Thinking™ at this stage, because at face value, it's possible that an idea still may not work. However, once they open their thinking to new possibilities like emerging packaging materials and technologies, new ingredient availability, new efficiency practices, etc., ideas can often be made profitable and feasible.

SUMMARY OF CHAPTER FOURTEEN – APPLYING CRITERIA #2 AND #3

1. Create a range of concepts or plans and apply Criteria #2 to each one with a simple "yes" or "no." If your answer is "no," adjust the communication until you can say "yes" to each criterion:
   - Breakthrough ideas?
   - Consistent treatment across concepts?
   - Concepts distinct from one another?
   - Single-minded communication?
   - A wide range of ideas from close-in to further out?
   - Desired blend of short-term, medium-term and long-term ideas?

2. Get your concepts/plans 80% perfect, and let your consumer/customer testing tell you how to adjust the idea to add the remaining 20%. Resist temptation to wordsmith ideas to death, because your consumers will change them anyway.

3. Determine profitability and feasibility ONLY on your top one or two ideas after testing. Don't be afraid to adjust the idea to make it profitable and feasible, as long as you aren't changing anything that is central to driving consumer/customer appeal.

TIPS FOR PERSONAL PROBLEM SOLVING

1. You won't be testing your ideas with consumers, customers or anyone else. Therefore it is up to YOU to select your top one or two ideas.

2. Criteria Set #2 is still helpful for you in evaluating your set of options; if you decide to adjust them somewhat, consider using:
    - I'm comfortable with how new and different each idea is.
    - All the options are viable options that, if followed, would solve my problem.
    - I have included options that solve my problem in different ways to increase my chance of success.
    - I have stretched my thinking far enough.
    - Each option is clear in my mind.

3. Feasibility is important for Criteria Set #3; remember to allow yourself the freedom to adjust any of your ideas to ensure they are feasible for you, personally.

TIPS FOR BUSINESS PROBLEM SOLVING

1. Truly great communication will make a big difference in the appeal of your ideas. If you work carefully with this set of criteria, you will have good communication.

2. The riskier the idea, the more consumer/customer testing you may need to justify the investment.

3. Do NOT allow your group to jump into profitability and feasibility until you have one or two winning ideas. It's a LOT of work to calculate these things for multiple ideas, and most of the time will be wasted on ideas consumers/customers didn't even like.

SECTION III:
TIPS AND GUIDELINES TO ENSURE SUCCESS

CHAPTER FIFTEEN

PLANNING YOUR CREATIVE PROBLEM SOLVING MEETING

Now is the time to put it all together. This chapter outlines how to plan and set up a meeting for a group of several people to work on solving a problem together. The following pages provide tips for doing it all yourself.

Let's go through the steps.

1. CONDUCT A CLIENT NEEDS ASSESSMENT

Begin with an in-depth discussion with your client, to answer the following questions:

- What is the business situation leading up to your need?
- What are the related issues?
- What has management been concerned about?
- What are you specifically trying to accomplish?

- Who is your target audience--new users? Existing users? Both?
- What do you want your audience to do as a result of this work?
- Who needs to be involved on the company side?
- What kind of end deliverables do you need?
- What are your next steps after this meeting?
- What is your budget?

Only when you know what you are working with—and not before—will you be able to figure out who must attend, how much time you need to solve the problem and when it should be scheduled.

2. CREATE YOUR PLAN

First, think about:

- What processes you'll use to solve the problem
- Who the key Stakeholders are
- How to get them in the room
- What your end deliverables will be
- Estimated timing and budget, where applicable.

Then write up your plan and share it with your team, to fine-tune and get their agreement. If you take the time to do this step, you and your participants will feel like you're on the same team, and the meeting itself will go more smoothly.

3. BOOK YOUR SESSION – FOUR HOURS MINIMUM!

Once you determine who needs to attend, check all calendars and book a date. This is important: Divergence and convergence require an equal amount of time; if you generate ideas for six hours, you will need a full six hours to select and develop your ideas.

Depending on the problem you're solving, plan no fewer than two hours for each step. Four or five hours for each step is even better.

Do NOT go for what I call the "businessman's special," that one-hour quickie session involving divergence only. While quick and painless, it's *always* a waste of time. The reason? Only top-of-mind ideas can be contributed in that short period of time—including all the obvious solutions your competitors have already identified, plus the obvious solutions your company has been batting around for years. And without convergence, you are left with a laundry list of undeveloped options, just flapping in the wind going nowhere, and will never see the light of day. It's a big waste of time and resources for all involved.

Instead, ensure your team takes the time it needs to get beyond the obvious to find innovative solutions that are defendable in the marketplace. It isn't until you start coming up with a few bad ideas that you know you've pushed your thinking as far as it can go.

4. FINALIZE YOUR ATTENDEES

Focusing on key stakeholders, including both internal management and external customers and prospects, create the guest list for your meeting. You may need to compensate any outsiders to incent them to attend. Also, pay careful attention to thinking styles, dominant and reserved personality styles, and levels of management in the room. Your goal is to create a diverse team of equals who all contribute from their own perspectives.

5. SECURE A MEETING ROOM AND GATHER EQUIPMENT

Be sure your meeting space is large enough to be comfortable for the number of people you have invited. Environment matters! If it's cozy, comfortable and relaxed, people will let their guards down and tap into their creative potential. If it's hot, cramped and high-pressure, with several levels of management attending and criticism flying, people will clam up and count down the minutes until they can bolt out of there!

Natural light and windows also add a lot to the atmosphere of a room, and can keep your team energized without much effort on your part. This is ideal if you have such a room available. If your available room is windowless, bring desk toys or pipe cleaners to put on all the tables -- I refer to these as "mindless manipulatives" that make your environment feel more fun and creative.

Arrange your room in a horseshoe shape with chairs only and no meeting tables. Provide clipboards and notepads for your participants. This creates an open, more exposed atmosphere that is highly productive for brainstorming. Participants sometimes feel a bit uncomfortable at the beginning, but this unique room arrangement clearly signals that this is not your usual meeting, and has the very real effect of opening up participants' minds.

Whenever possible, try to seat everyone in the room in the same style of chair to level the playing field and set an atmosphere of equality. One "special" chair for the top manager in the room kills the inclusive feeling we are trying to create.

Be sure to secure *two* flip charts, each with lots of paper, and bring colored markers and masking tape to post flip chart pages as needed. Having two allows you to post instructions on one chart, while recording ideas on the other.

I do not recommend using white boards because the room quickly looks chaotic, and key information often must be erased to make room for the next section of the meeting. Using old fashioned paper allows you to keep your output organized, and make sure nothing falls through the cracks.

Better yet, find a real-time typist who can record every idea as it's expressed, and project them all on a screen for the room to follow. If you are able to find someone smart enough and fast enough to keep up, you'll only need one paper flip chart for creative activities or to jot down instructions.

6. PLAN ACTIVITIES AND GATHER SUPPLIES

Think of your meeting plan as being "broad brush" and flexible. Right now your objective is to plan fairly large time blocks with potential activities and list the associated materials or supplies you'll need—we won't know which excursions fit best until we've identified themes or territories, so we need to be prepared for whatever topics come up.

For this reason, we always plan at least ten more exercises than we know we have time for, to allow us the flexibility to shift activities around, depending on the needs of the team at the moment. The day often flows according to the following large time blocks:

Timing	Activity	Supplies & Notes
9:00am-9:15am	Team Introductions	Name, Department, Something you're looking forward to
9:15am-10:30am	Wishing	Homework Assignment
10:30am-11:00am	Identify Territories	Flip Chart, note pads
11:00am-Noon	Territory #1	Role Play worksheets
Noon-1:00pm	Lunch	Catering; check team allergies
1:00pm-2:00pm	Territory #2	Word Associations List
2:00pm-3:00pm	Territory #3	Get Fired Idea, trade papers with partner
Etc.		

Assuming we are addressing "How to make our business more efficient," our additional "back pocket" activities we are ready to conduct if needed may include:

1. Picture Cards Activity: find "efficiency" in your picture
2. Voyage to Planet Efficiency: fantasy exercise
3. Paired Activity: customer-company role play
4. Extreme/Get Fired: pass to the person on your right
5. Customer Complaints List: shout out the list and solve efficiency issues
6. Associations with "Efficiency": make list together
7. Triangle Exercise: customer type – other words for efficiency – product line
8. Worlds Excursion: find a metaphorical example of efficiency
9. Wallet/Backpack Grab Bag Object: force fit to "efficiency"
10. Tech Geek Catalogs to find efficiency related benefits we can apply to our business

See Chapter 9: Excursion Theory

7. DO NOT FORGET THE REFRESHMENTS!

We have discovered over the years that a strong correlation exists between food and great ideas. For example, right before lunch, stomachs rumble and energy wanes, while immediately following our afternoon snack the room is in high gear. We recommend you provide beverages and snacks—at the bare minimum—to keep blood sugar steady and ideas flowing. Most essential are lots of water for good hydration, natural sugars like fresh fruit and veggies, and protein like raw nuts. If you're able to provide breakfast and lunch too, all the better.

You can even use processed sugar strategically to put your group in high gear for a "lightening round" of brainstorming. But I would recommend you use it sparingly because sugar crashes can kill the energy in the room after your lightening round is over.

It may sound silly, but trust me—serving refreshments will make a difference in your productivity!

SUMMARY OF CHAPTER FIFTEEN – PLANNING YOUR CREATIVE PROBLEM SOLVING MEETING

1. Conduct a thorough needs assessment first, and take the time to ask your client contact enough questions to truly nail down what they want to accomplish and how much risk they are willing to take.

2. Once you are clear on all the objectives, create a detailed plan, but keep it broad-brush and stay flexible. Planning thoroughly allows you to pivot in the moment.

3. Allow enough time to get past the obvious ideas and into truly innovative territory. Plan an equal amount of time for diverging and converging.

4. Create a warm and open environment for ideas to flourish by securing a room large enough to set up in a horseshoe arrangement with chairs only—no tables—and clipboards.

5. Provide refreshments to keep energy up and ideas flowing.

TIPS FOR PERSONAL PROBLEM SOLVING

1. You may want to include only a few, very close people to help you solve your problem. If this is the case, consider using someone's living room or other warm and comfortable environment.

2. Work on paper with pen or pencil instead of flip charts.

3. Give yourself an equal amount of time to diverge and converge, and allow at least two hours for each step, to ensure you have an opportunity for full exploration of options.

TIPS FOR BUSINESS PROBLEM SOLVING

1. Facilitating CPS appears to be very easy to the untrained eye, because it looks like a teacher standing in front of the room with a marker, simply writing down what other people say. However, there is a LOT more to it, including: managing group dynamics, choosing and facilitating creative activities that make brainstorming easy for the group, managing time, identifying and maintaining strategic focus, monitoring the quality of ideas, keeping ideas on topic and so much more. Plan thoroughly.

2. The more you have planned, the easier it will be to flex with the topics that emerge and the in-the-moment decisions the team makes.

3. Be prepared to lead many, many more excursions than you could possibly have time for, to make sure you pull the best excursion out at the best time to deliver the best possible ideas.

CHAPTER SIXTEEN

CREATING THE IDEAL CREATIVE PROBLEM SOLVING TEAM

Creative problem solving works extremely well in groups because each participant brings a unique perspective. Going back to the key principles in the Osborne-Parnes CPS model, we know that diversity of perspectives is a key element, and diversity comes from working with a group. In any given group, each individual has grown up in a different household with different parents and siblings, had different experiences, learned from different teachers who inspired them, lived in different regions, embraced different cultures and made different day-to-day life choices.

Harnessing this diversity of perspectives allows for a 360-degree approach to problem solving with each participant chipping away at the problem from a different vantage point. This is why role-playing can be such a powerful tool for brainstorming — if, for example, I imagine for a moment that I am my mother, I guarantee I will express needs, likes and ideas that are different from what I would express when speaking from my own perspective.

You can capitalize on the power of diversity by inviting others into your brainstorming session, whether you are focusing on a personal problem or a business problem. If your problem is personal, you may want to include only close confidantes with whom you are comfortable sharing your issue and ideas. When working with a business problem, your team members can help.

WHO ARE THE BEST PEOPLE TO INCLUDE?

1. Your End Customer or Consumer

Put the strongest emphasis on including your end user—the party who needs to "buy" the solution, both figuratively and literally. If you begin with the needs of end users (your customer or consumer, for example), your chances of success increase significantly.

It's natural to focus on ourselves and our product or our service, because we know ourselves and our businesses better than anyone else does. However, company leaders and employees can forget that even though they, personally, live and breathe their product every day, people who use the product are usually not as invested—and they are the people who matter most. Resist the temptation to drink the Kool-Aid of corporate groupthink; if your consumers tell you, "I really don't care that much…it's only toilet paper," believe them! They really *don't* care the way you do, and nothing you can say will change that.

If you are working on a personal problem, the end user is YOU. Therefore, your needs should be the focus.

2. <u>Key Stakeholders</u>

In addition to your end user(s), find people who have some stake in the solution—your key stakeholders. To do this, take a 360-degree look at all the types of people surrounding the issue. In a business setting, that may include the management team, cross-functional managers, your current and prospective customers, your consumers, etc. Think about who will participate in executing the resulting ideas—they also must buy into the solution and be on board with team direction.

Cross-functional team members can include people from various departments like Sales, Finance, R&D, Operations, Market Research/Consumer Insights, Sensory Testing, Branding, Promotions, etc. Select ONE person from each key area relevant to your business problem.

The Benefit: Inclusive idea creation ensures organizational commitment to the resulting ideas because all executors collaborated to create one comprehensive solution.

When addressing a personal problem such as "How to get my family of five to school and work in the morning without chaos or conflicts," stakeholders might include: mom and dad, kids, school bus driver, the next door neighbor who stands at the bus stop with the kids, and nanny and grandma—the two morning preschool drivers.

The Benefit: Sitting down together to brainstorm solutions to morning chaos is a very effective way to solve a problem and arrive at solutions that work for everyone involved.

Remember to reward those who lend their time to you, such as the school bus driver and the next door neighbor. Sometimes nice refreshments are all that is needed to say, "Thank you for helping me." If you can't or don't want to serve refreshments, a small gift card to a grocery or coffee shop can be a nice thank you gift as well.

3. Those With Diverse Perspectives

The ideal participants in creative problem solving bring unique perspectives on the issue and opportunity. In addition to cross-functional team members, other participants can be helpful, too.

Sometimes we throw in a "wild card" participant—someone who is irrelevant to the issue but known to be highly creative. If a problem is not too technical or complex, kids and teens are great wild card contributors because they provide a naïve perspective that often zeroes in on the key issues. Another type of wild card participant to pursue is the subject-matter expert, such as a chef for food innovation, or a writer for entertainment innovation. Or you can include a great creative thinker with no prior knowledge of the problem—an artist, actor, musician, poet, etc.

The Benefit: greater diversity yields a richer range of ideas; diversity also allows for many facets of the problem to be addressed simultaneously to facilitate comprehensive solutions that truly work.

HOW MANY PEOPLE SHOULD BE INCLUDED?

1. No More Than Eight for a Live Session

The ideal number of participants for a live creative problem solving session is six to eight, to ensure that everyone involved has plenty of time to think, and plenty of airtime to contribute ideas. More people means less talk time for each individual. And while fewer than six will work, there is a tradeoff between providing airtime and gaining diversity of perspectives.

Resist the temptation to involve a huge team. The more people you are facilitating, the more chaotic the session can seem, unless you use advanced techniques not covered in this book. And in my experience, chaotic sessions make business people very uncomfortable! If that happens, they're unlikely to want to repeat the process on another issue and may be suspect of the meeting outcome.

2. <u>Unlimited Number of Participants for an Online Session</u>

If you want to include more people for the purpose of building consensus within the organization, consider using an idea database to collect ideas. This allows for an unlimited number of participants who won't have to wait their turn to contribute ideas. This also has the advantage of collecting ideas anonymously, which automatically creates that important level playing field.

If you decide to conduct an online session, be aware that teammates tend to check in and out of the process as their schedules permit; furthermore, they may not be as fully invested in the process as compared to a live session. This is sometimes a worthwhile tradeoff because online sessions are fast and efficient. However, if you are relying on your team to make timely decisions in order to keep the process moving forward — such as which territories they are most interested in pursuing — be aware that you may need to build in additional time to hold team discussions.

One final word about online idea generation: As I mentioned earlier in the credit card / pregnancy anecdote, online brainstorming must be tightly managed and facilitated to prevent drifting into off-topic issues.

WHAT QUALITIES ARE WE LOOKING FOR IN PARTICIPANTS?

1. <u>People with knowledge</u> of the end users' needs. End users themselves are best, but facsimiles can be used when that's impractical; participants such as sales reps, customer service reps, call center employees, remote regional managers, etc. can all be helpful in representing the end user if needed.

2. <u>People with responsibility for executing the solution</u> chosen by the team, and who must therefore agree to the solution to ensure it is supported versus hindered. This is the all-important "buy-in."

3. <u>Non-linear thinkers</u>, whenever possible — the more lateral thinkers you include, the easier it will be to create a range of new ideas. Refer to Chapter Three on Thinking Styles.

What should you do if you can't decide between a strong, linear-thinking stakeholder and a lateral-thinking non-stakeholder? Go with the stakeholder. Creating ideas will be more difficult, but the ones you do create are much more likely to see the light of day.

CHAPTER SIXTEEN SUMMARY – THE IDEAL CREATIVE PROBLEM SOLVING TEAM

1. Due to diversity of perspectives, brainstorming and problem solving are very effective when treated as a team sport.

2. For personal problems, choose one or two people you truly trust and ask them to help you.

3. For business problems, provide a 360-degree perspective by including your end user, key stakeholders and a cross-functional team with diverse perspectives.

TIPS FOR PERSONAL PROBLEM SOLVING

1. Some problems are so personal you may want to work alone and do your best to chip away at it yourself, without assistance from others.

2. If you possibly can, find someone you trust completely, and share the problem with him or her. Two heads are better than one and three heads are better than two, because the others give you a new point of view.

3. If your personal problem naturally involves others, such as "How to organize our family's activities better," bring in all those involved in the challenge to work together on a solution that fits everyone's needs.

TIPS FOR BUSINESS PROBLEM SOLVING

1. Include and focus on the needs of end users, who are literally or figuratively "buying" your solution.

2. Include key stakeholders who must buy into the ultimate solution in order for you to sell it up the line and execute it with excellence.

3. Once you have identified the people with the right responsibilities, try to secure some lateral thinkers to make your brainstorming job easier. Lateral thinkers are quicker to suspend judgment and are more likely to come up with many ideas for solving a problem.

CHAPTER SEVENTEEN

IN-MEETING TIPS TO ENSURE YOUR SUCCESS

Now that your meeting is planned and participants are scheduled and committed to your session, it's time to examine a few tips and guidelines to help the session go smoothly.

We learned all of these lessons the hard way-- by making mistakes and experiencing the consequences of our poor decisions. With a focus on continuous improvement, however, we adjusted our process each time we made a mistake to prevent it from occurring in the future. So, learn from our mistakes and get it right the first time around!

1. START BY ASSIGNING THE ROLE OF KEY CLIENT.

- Identify the person on the team who has the greatest strategic responsibility for making something happen with results of the project. Often this is the marketing person leading the innovation or problem solving effort.

- Explain that this person acts as leader of the team, sharing information as needed to clarify their objectives and steering meeting content to ensure we are always focusing on the right ideas. This person also acts as "tie-breaker" in the event the team is evenly split on an issue and a decision must be made to keep the project moving forward.

2. ALWAYS START WITH A KICKOFF MEETING TO SET CLEAR EXPECTATIONS; MAKE IT MANDATORY FOR ALL PARTICIPANTS.

Ask for introductions and expectations.

- Start the day with introductions and project expectations. Ask participants to introduce themselves by stating their name, their role on the team and what they hope to get out of the project.

- Jot down participant expectations so you can address them directly. Be clear on what will and will not be accomplished during the session; by setting clear expectations, everyone will be on board and moving in the same direction. In addition, you'll have increased client satisfaction after the project is over because you've met everyone's expectations.

- Any expectations that will not be met during the live session should be recorded on a "Parking Lot" flip chart page. This page collects key issues to be addressed later and ensures all participants are heard. This also ensures the session isn't thrown off track by tangential issues and time-wasting debates and discussions.

Post the purpose statement and describe end deliverables.

- Prepare a purpose statement and show it to the team, asking participants to correct, add to, delete from or change it in any way. When team members suggest changes, check in with the Key Client before editing the statement, to make sure it fits the team's strategic objectives.

- Be very clear about what the team will walk away with — a ranked list of ideas to work through? A range of concepts ready for consumer testing? Action plans to take to Product Development for additional vetting? Whatever it is, be clear about what you will deliver and when the team will receive it. In the end, they will be more satisfied with the project results because you'll always deliver what they expect.

Clarify project scope.

- To ensure your team agrees on how far they want to stretch their thinking, draw a circular "Scope Rope" and ask a series of questions about what's off limits and what's in scope. As you ask each question, record the answers either inside or outside of the loop.

- Simply having this discussion with the team enables them to stretch as far as they want, while ensuring all ideas are in scope as per team objectives. It also clearly defines what the team wants and does not want, which puts everyone on the same page so they can work together toward the goal.

Describe roles and responsibilities.

Be clear on who is attending and what you want each person to do during the session. If you are bringing in outsiders such as subject matter experts, customers or end consumers, make sure they are sharing ideas from their own perspectives, to provide a different view of the issues.

Be particularly clear on what you want the client team to do. We suggest they:

- Generate a quantity of ideas.
- Build on ideas of outside experts and consumers, to ensure ideas also meet the company's needs.
- Suspend judgment until convergence begins.
- Refrain from debating ideas or discussing tangential topics.
- Use Greenhouse Thinking™ to find what's good within an idea, and to build wishes to improve the idea.
- Refrain from note-taking, because all ideas are being recorded by the leader or typist, and note-taking is almost always evaluation in disguise!

Plan the process you'll be using and create an outline.

While it is difficult to perfectly predict an agenda with tight time blocks, explain your process in stages vs. time blocks—that provides flexibility to work longer on some topics than others, depending on the strategic needs of the team.

At bare minimum, outline the "diamond" of diverging, followed by converging (see page 20.)

Spend at least 20 minutes on Greenhouse Thinking™.

Explain the rules of engagement for creating a positive mindset and allow your team to practice Greenhouse Thinking on a crazy, off-topic idea. When you work off-topic, your team can have fun with the exercise because it's just a wild example, and no one is invested in the outcome. Some ideas we've used as ridiculous examples in the past include:

- Human Carwash—do-it-yourself conveyor-belt bathing for the whole family
- Mink-covered shower stalls
- Family homes made of LEGOs®

You can also make up your own ridiculous idea and share it with your team. Ask them to list everything they like about the idea first. Then ask them what they wish for to improve the idea. Once the exercise is complete, quickly explain why we ask teams to play along by sharing the benefit of Greenhouse Thinking™ described in Chapter Four.

Wrap up your kickoff with the following guidelines to make the process run smoothly:

- <u>Write ideas down</u>.

    Tell your team that because ideas are fleeting, it's important to write them down as soon as they occur. That way, you have retained the first idea and freed yourself to listen in again and create a new idea.

    If you don't write them down you will either lose them—sometimes never to be found again—or work so hard to hang onto them that you have no brain space to come up with more new ideas.

Once you write down an idea, you've got it. Then get another idea.

- <u>Headline your ideas.</u>

   Just like in a news story, a headline shares the essence of the story; if you want more information, you can always read further. Please contribute all your ideas in headline form, including enough information for someone reading the idea later to understand it, but not so much that the idea gets lost in the detail.

   Resist temptation to tell the back story to your idea, or to sell it. Both just eat up time and contribute nothing new.

   Here is what NOT to do: "My nephew is coming to visit and he is so adorable. And last summer I watched him play with his toys and he had a set of rings that he was fascinated with—stacking and unstacking the rings. I watched for a long time, and that made me think we should make our new snacks stackable ring shapes.

   As entertaining as my nephew's story might (or might not!) be, there is nothing helpful about sharing it. We only want to hear, "Make the snacks stackable ring shapes."

   Here is another example of what NOT to do: "We should make the snack stackable ring shapes because our competitors are all square; our production line prefers ring-shaped items because the line moves faster that way; and one of our big customers asked if we could change the product to make it stackable rings"

This is selling the idea, and all we need to hear is "Make the snacks round." That, and that alone, is the headline.

- Focus on producing a quantity of ideas.

    Often teams come to believe that an idea must be perfect before it can be shared. Perhaps they've been in one too many idea-killing meetings. Be very clear that *quality comes from quantity* in this brainstorming game. Let them know that imperfect ideas can be volleyed to teammates to build on and improve, and can spark a new idea for someone else.

    Once the team understands that quantity is king, they will feel much freer to toss an idea out that is not perfect but could be helpful.

- Remind the group to practice In-and-Out Listening.

    Instructions are: "Listen in to find something that creates a spark for you, then stop listening and use the other side of your brain to create a new idea. Record the idea on your paper, and then listen in again for something else that sparks an idea."

As you can see from the content of this meeting, team attendance must be mandatory. If you don't make the kickoff mandatory, many people will choose to skip it and then become disruptive during the session because they aren't clear on rules of engagement and expectations. In addition, those who missed it are working at a disadvantage compared to their prepared teammates, and that can be an uncomfortable situation for the latecomer.

3. BEGIN WISHING... AND ENFORCE ALL RULES FROM THE START.

If someone on your team has a side conversation, stop it immediately by asking, "Sorry to interrupt, but are you discussing something the whole team should hear?" If so, they will share it with the team. If not, they will immediately stop talking.

If someone expresses dislike for an idea, immediately ask, "What do you *wish for* to solve that problem?" Do NOT allow negative discussions to take place; nip them in the bud the moment they begin. Whatever you do early in the session sets a precedence for the rest of the session, so correcting now prevents issues for you later.

By the same token when you ask someone to change their objection to a wish, wait for them to come up with something and then record the idea—even if it takes them a moment. This not only helps the offender understand what to do next time, it also illustrates for the entire team how to turn negative thoughts to positive contributions.

4. MANAGE TIMING AND BREAKS LIKE A PRO.

Your start times, end times and lunch time are all "hard stops"—no matter what happens during the day, set a clear expectation that you always start exactly on time and stop exactly on time, so the team can make their plans accordingly.

Then, enforce this timing rigorously—people will be late once but not a second time!

Here is a great little secret about break time: Announce your breaks in specific times versus round numbers, and people will return to the room exactly on time! For example, instead of saying, "Let's take a ten-minute break," try announcing, "Let's take an 11-minute break."

5. RECORD ALL IDEAS ACCURATELY, TO THE SATISFACTION OF THE IDEA CONTRIBUTOR.

- As the facilitator, you are NOT the editor. Holding that marker comes with great responsibility to accurately record each idea so that it remains true to the intention of the contributor.

- Nothing is more upsetting to a participant than to share an idea that is never written down. When that happens the participant hears, "That was a stupid idea, not worth recording." You will find that if you do this, the room will slowly but surely shut down, and you will stop hearing ideas from everyone.

- By the same token if you paraphrase an idea to save space on your chart, check in with the contributor immediately before moving on to make sure you have recorded it to that person's satisfaction. If necessary, rewrite it until the contributor is satisfied. Taking a moment to do this says to your team, "Every idea is very important and valued, so please help keep me honest in creating *your* idea list. I am just the idea handler, not the decision maker."

6. KEEP YOUR REDIRECTION LIGHT-HANDED AND POSITIVE.

As the leader, you must keep your group under control and working productively toward the goal. There are several ways to keep your leadership positive, even while correcting unproductive behavior.

Make a joke.

When you do need to correct behavior and ask a participant to redirect to a task, make a joke at your own expense if you can, to lighten the correction. For example, if you hear a team member chatting in the hallway about the project and potentially breaching confidentiality rules, you can say, "I'm sorry—when we talked about confidentiality, I forgot to mention: The doorway to our meeting room is magical and erases your memory when you exit, and then magically restores your memory when you re-enter! That way no one can accidentally be overheard and risk breaching confidentiality. Did you feel it when you walked through?"

Praise good behavior.

Another way to redirect is to praise behavior you want to see. If participants are getting a bit off course, don't shut them down by calling them out on it. Instead, wait until you've called on a few more people and then praise an idea that is back on course with a comment like, "You're right on target for what the team is looking for, and we'd love to hear more ideas like that one."

Correct the team in general, not the individual.

Here is another great light-handed technique that positively redirects behavior. Go around the semi-circle to collect a range of ideas and then contribute one of your own. Right after you've said your new idea, check in with the client and ask, "Are these the kinds of ideas you were hoping for, or would you like to redirect the team in any way?" Coax your client to tell you what they want done differently in a positive way—for example, "We're interested in all-family ideas more than kid-specific ideas, so I'd like to stay focused on the family."

This is much more positive than saying, "We have way too many kid-specific ideas and the law prohibits us from targeting them directly, so no more kid stuff!!"

Praise ideas regularly.

Unlike during a focus group, where we try not to bias the respondents, it's important to praise new ideas because the encouragement keeps them coming. Freely use the expressions, "Great!" or "Good one!" or "Wow, nice one!" Even a more modest, "Good!" or a nod of your head with a positive expression on your face can be helpful.

If you aren't clear about the meaning of an idea being expressed by a participant, or you believe your broader team might not know what they mean, ask non-leading follow-up questions such as, "Say more, please" or "Help me understand what's behind that idea" or "Can you elaborate?"

7. USE SUBTLE BODY LANGUAGE TO CONTROL THE ROOM.

Many techniques can help you maintain tight control of your session without anyone else being aware of it.

Turn your shoulder to control a dominator.
If someone in the room keeps stealing the floor, very gently and subtly turn your shoulder away from that person; you aren't turning your body completely, just making a slight shift to give another person eye contact. Then call on that person and others on that side of the room for a few minutes. The dominator will get the message without any embarrassment.

Occasionally go around the room in order.

Introverts prefer to process information silently in their heads and then announce an answer. Extroverts prefer to think out loud, to figure out what they think. That's why different people will behave differently in a session—some waiting quietly for a turn, while others shout out ideas. We value ALL contributions, so it's important to periodically go around the room in turn. That gives everyone equal airtime and quiets the blurters to give others a chance to share their ideas.

Walk into the center of the semi-circle to stop chatter.

When participants start having side conversations, it may be time for you to call a short bio-break. To stop it quickly, just take one or two steps closer to the people who are chatting and catch the eye of one of them. Then call on someone across the room to share an idea. The talkers will instantly stop without feeling scolded.

You will find over time that if you practice these tips and guidelines, it won't be long before you are facilitating like a pro. And as with everything else, practice makes perfect.

SUMMARY OF CHAPTER SEVENTEEN – IN-MEETING TIPS TO ENSURE YOUR SUCCESS

1. Assign the role of the Key Client to establish strategic leadership and ensure decisions are made in a timely way, to keep the project moving forward.

2. Begin the day with team introductions and expectations, and make sure you address all expectations either during your meeting or within a "Parking Lot" of issues.

3. Start with a Mandatory Project Kickoff to align the team and set clear expectations, including:
    - Purpose and Deliverables
    - Project Scope
    - Roles and Responsibilities
    - Process
    - Greenhouse Environment/Rules of Engagement
    - Tips and Guidelines

4. Begin wishing and immediately correct any unproductive behavior that emerges—if you don't, this behavior will haunt you for the rest of the session. Use the light-handed techniques above.

TIPS FOR PERSONAL PROBLEM SOLVING

1. You are unlikely to have a meeting at all; I would recommend you focus instead on Chapter Nineteen: Doing It All Yourself

2. While you're unlikely to ever conduct a kickoff meeting, you may find it helpful to go through the steps yourself, to make sure you are heading in the direction you want to go.

TIPS FOR BUSINESS PROBLEM SOLVING

1. Some of the steps outlined in this section can be difficult for an internal manager to facilitate, because disagreeing with upper managers who determine your future employment involves risk. In that case, consider bringing in an outside facilitator who will be treated as a neutral leader, especially if the topic is controversial.

2. Practice your kickoff in advance to make sure it goes smoothly; there are many details to impart, and it can be hard to remember them all if you haven't practiced.

3. Err on the side of being too light-handed in your control of the group, and allow a *little bit* of chaos. You don't want to risk being too heavy-handed and offending someone, or accidentally create a high pressure environment for your team.

CHAPTER EIGHTEEN

GROUP DYNAMICS CHALLENGES

Working with a team is dynamic, multi-faceted and synergistic when it comes to creative problem solving. It also presents its challenges, especially if you have some resisters in the room.

This chapter outlines several different types of team members, the challenges their points of view create for the larger group, and suggestions for managing group dynamics in a way that is fun, light-handed, keeps you on track and brings out the best in every single participant.

A quick note before we dive in: I have used the pronoun "he" simply because it gets cumbersome to say "he or she" repeatedly. The truth is, the vast majority of my clients over the years have been women. It would be a bit more correct for me to use "she" throughout this explanation of group dynamics, but grammar conventions call for "he".

With that said, here are some of the participant styles I have encountered over the years.

THE EGO

This type of person believes he is the only one in the room, or at least the only one in the room who matters. Sometimes this person is the top dog in the group, but sometimes he's not. You can tell by his title and the title of the others in your group.

If he is the top dog, you must take his direction, and it doesn't hurt to fan his ego a little more by praising his brilliant ideas. If he isn't top dog, your job is to make sure he gets the same amount of airtime—and not more—than anyone else. To do this, you can use body posture to slightly turn your back to him and call on another person. Then, be sure to call him by name when his turn comes back around. We don't want him to mentally drop out of the meeting, but we do want to get ideas from everyone in the room, including him.

THE SABOTEUR

This person never bought into the project plan in the first place and may believe that an approach other than CPS would work better. Often people like this have been at the company a long time and come with a lot of history and, therefore, clout. They may have been left out of the process to decide on a project plan and often come from R&D, Operations or Marketing Management, where they have become firmly grounded in immediate feasibility and have "seen it all before."

My best example of the Saboteur was an R&D executive who had been at a window blind company for 40 years. He knew it all and was angry that no one had asked his opinion prior to embarking on the CPS process, so he proceeded to trash every idea anyone else came up with, incorporating long stories about how in 1969 the company had tried that idea and it didn't work then, so it wouldn't work now.

After the facilitator had made several light-handed jokes and covered the Saboteur's shirt in "I wish" stickers to remind him to think positively, his behavior became truly destructive to the project and disrespectful to the team. In the end we had to be kind, direct and firm—when he began to object, I simply cut him off and redirected by asking, "What do you wish for instead?" We used this approach with him repeatedly, but he couldn't or wouldn't create any new wishes or ideas and eventually gave up. It was a shame to lose his potential contributions, but it was more important to stop his negativity.

THE PASSIVE AGGRESSIVE MASTER

This is the participant who *seems* to go along with everything, but waits until it's all over to kill the project. If this person is the top dog, you may be in trouble. Recently, I conducted a month-long session for a technology company. The session began with audience needs research; moved into consumer co-creation, concept development and focus groups; and proceeded to development of rapid prototypes for the best ideas. Unfortunately, the head of Marketing came to the first meeting but skipped the others. One month after the project closed this leader threw out all that work (and a lot of money!), and is now taking a few steps back and rethinking the whole issue. She had decided months ago that she did not support the CPS effort.

If a participant like this is not the top dog, we can ignore his passive aggressive nature. As long as he contributes constructively in session, we can produce a great result. One great thing about Passive Aggressive Masters: They *appear* to be cooperative!

THE MOUSE

Working with the Mouse is not difficult at all—he can hardly be heard when he speaks and is frequently asked to repeat himself so everyone can hear. The Mouse contributes nothing if unprompted, and never raises his hand or volunteers ideas or information. The Mouse is often a lower-level employee who is too afraid to offer ideas, especially with two levels of higher management in the room at the same time.

Working with the Mouse simply requires building his confidence and helping him understand the importance of his perspective. And his perspective truly is important because he is the one who is closest to the front line, analyzing the data regularly and keeping his fingers on the pulse of the business. If he interacts directly with customers, he also knows how they think and what they care about most.

To help the Mouse express his ideas, call on him directly even if his hand isn't raised. Give him more incubation time, because he is likely to be an introvert who prefers to process information silently. Then praise whatever idea he contributes. For example, you can say, "Interesting idea! Anyone else have any builds on that?" A simple word or two in the right place can bring the Mouse into the fold as a full participant.

Surprisingly, sometimes the top dog is mistaken for the Mouse. If he's great at his job, a good manager of people and confident in himself and his place in the company, the top dog can be the most unimposing figure in the room. But trust me—he is no Mouse! On the contrary, he is simply a great leader who truly delegates and values the expertise of his staff and team.

THE PLEASER

It's really fun working with the Pleaser. This type of participant is also known as a "yes man," who frequently agrees with anyone and everyone, yet offers nothing new. Working with this type of participant is always positive. He loves everything! What's not to like?

If the top dog in your brainstorming session is a Pleaser, he may not be very decisive or discerning. When this difficulty emerges during a session, your job is to provide him with two clear options, offer a brief explanation of the tradeoffs between the two and then ask for a decision. If he still resists, call a short team meeting and ask the other team members to weigh in on the choices.

Here is a concrete example: I was in a session earlier this year with a leader who was a Pleaser. We needed a decision on whether we should focus on ideas that appeal to the whole family, or opt for ideas that appeal to kids specifically. He just couldn't decide because he wanted all his teammates to be happy with the decision. So we opened discussion with the broader team and asked for their opinions. Then, I summarized with this: "It sounds to me like the team believes the bigger opportunity lies in all family ideas. Is that ok with you?" And what did the Pleaser say? Why, "YES!" Of course!

If your Pleaser is not the top dog, just run with it as usual. He will be a very pleasant addition to your team, acting as cheerleader for everyone else's brilliant thinking.

THE BLACK CLOUD

I think we all know someone who serves as a bit of a Black Cloud, always pointing out the negative in any situation. This type can find a problem with anything and everything, even in the face of happy events like celebrations and great human achievements. Saturday Night Live spoofed this personality type several years ago with a character they called "Debbie Downer." Everything she said was negative, and each time she spoke it was followed by two musical tones in a minor key. "Whaaaa, whaaaa…"

Whether your Black Cloud is the top dog or a participant, the approach is the same: Give this person a thorough explanation of Greenhouse Thinking™ and enforce the rules throughout your session. When addressing any negative, ask this participant what he LIKES about the idea, and require him to respond with at least three things. Then ask, "What do you wish for instead?" Don't let him wiggle out of it; instead, push him to say something –anything— positive. By keeping the Black Cloud focused on an Open Mindset, you will help him get into the habit of saying what he *wants* instead of what he doesn't want. Just that simple shift in thinking can change a person's outlook.

THE DIPLOMAT

This person has a velvet tongue, with every word carefully chosen to convey his precise meaning. He wants everyone to get along, but accomplishes this through leadership rather than glad-handing. Often your top dog is the quintessential Diplomat. And he didn't get to where he is by ticking people off—his way with words and egalitarian manner have propelled him to leadership.

When working with the Diplomat, your key challenge will be to understand what he *truly* wants out of the session, which may or may not be what he says he wants. By asking a series of neutral but targeted questions about his overall goals, the ideal outcome of the session and next steps, you can break through all the diplomacy and deliver exactly what he needs.

Others in the group who play the Diplomat are also easy to work with. They tend to be positive, constructive and contributive—as such, they add a lot to the positive spirit of the team.

THE KNOW-IT-ALL

This type of participant is quite a character and a force to be reckoned with! The Know-it-All comes in two forms: the one who really *does* know it all because he's been around forever, and the one who just *thinks* he knows it all, because he is young, immature and a bit on the arrogant side.

The real Know-it-All can be a lot like the Saboteur, because he truly has seen and done it all during his tenure with the company. This participant type is weighted down with too much knowledge. How can a person have "too much knowledge" you may ask? The truth is, the more you know about any given subject, the harder it is to think of new ideas. As your knowledge grows, you get more boxed in than ever.

To handle the real Know-It-All, remind him frequently to suspend judgment during the divergent portion of the project, and reassure him that he will have plenty of time to evaluate ideas during convergence. If he tries to voice objections, quickly counter with, "What do you wish for to overcome your objection?" Also remind him that ideas sometimes fail because the time isn't right. Something that didn't work in 1986 may work today.

The participant who simply *thinks* he knows it all is much easier to deal with—he is acting superior because he feels insecure in his position. Give this participant extra encouragement, and simply ignore any pompous behavior.

THE PUPPETEER

I've saved my favorite participant type for last. The Puppeteer is the team leader who wants to delegate, who wishes he could delegate, but really just pretends to delegate. This person designates a leader and then overrides every decision by pulling strings from behind the scenes. The Puppeteer can be hard to spot at first because he seems like a strong and secure leader. Once he begins reversing decisions behind the scenes, however, his identity becomes clear.

To work with the Puppeteer you must recognize him for who he is—the key decision maker. Instead of taking direction from his designated leader as you were asked to do, you must always check in with him because he is the only real decision-maker. When his designated leader makes a call, run it by the Puppeteer every time to confirm he agrees. If you don't, each decision will be quickly reversed and you will waste a lot of time.

As you can see, team dynamics add another layer to every creative problem solving session. It's important to set clear expectations up front and explain all the rules of engagement, so you won't need to correct behavior later. The more positive you can be in your facilitation, the more enjoyable and productive your session will be for everyone.

SUMMARY OF CHAPTER EIGHTEEN – GROUP DYNAMICS CHALLENGES

1. There are many different participant personality styles; your challenge is to "read" styles within the team so you can keep everyone on track and feeling positive.

2. Common personality styles I've come across include:
    a. The Ego
    b. The Saboteur
    c. The Passive Aggressive Master
    d. The Mouse
    e. The Pleaser
    f. The Diplomat
    g. The Know-It-All
    h. The Puppeteer

3. Each type requires different facilitation skills and brings unique challenges to group dynamics.

4. Set clear expectations up front so that any subsequent finessing of group dynamics will be light-handed and light-hearted, to keep the group enthusiastic and engaged.

TIPS FOR PERSONAL PROBLEM SOLVING

1. Review these personality types and see if any of them apply to you.

2. If you find one that does, pay attention to the pitfalls of that type, so you can work to avoid them.

TIPS FOR BUSINESS PROBLEM SOLVING

1. When you first try this out, just do your best. Great managers of group dynamics are made, not born.

2. As you gather more experience over time, hone your skills in managing the various types and make note of any new types that emerge from your session.

3. When in doubt, always make a positive comment to redirect non-productive behavior. For example, instead of saying, "You're being negative right now," say, "Interesting point! What do you wish for to overcome your concern?" Alternatively, call out good behavior when you see it by saying, for example, "Adam has opened up some new options with his idea for (blank); who else has an idea like that one?"

CHAPTER NINETEEN
DOING IT ALL YOURSELF

There are a few reasons you may want to do your Creative Problem Solving yourself:

- If it's a personal problem that you don't want to share with others
- If it's a business problem and no one else shares the issue, so it's up to you to solve it
- If it's a highly confidential business problem that must be kept secret for competitive reasons
- If you want to set yourself apart from peers by being more innovative day-to-day
- If your team shares the issue, but your teammates don't have the time or resources to participate in creating solutions, so they delegate it to you

There may be other reasons as well; regardless of why you're working alone, however, the following steps may help you.

IDENTIFY YOUR PROBLEM

Before you determine which problem you want to address, create a long list of "How to" statements that reflect the problem from many angles. Challenge yourself to create at least ten different statements.

To use an example from my own life, I might choose to solve the problem, "How to get my kids to put their laundry in the basket every time—instead of leaving laundry all over the house." "How to" statements might include:

1. How to get all clothes in the basket as soon as they're taken off
2. How to make the task fun
3. How to teach my kids responsibility
4. How to make my life easier
5. How to keep my house clean enough to avoid feeling stressed
6. How to teach my kids the importance of tidiness
7. How to show my kids that they should value their possessions
8. How to develop consequences for my kids when they don't do what I've asked
9. How to teach neatness to my entire family including the adults in my home
10. How to delegate laundry hassles to others
11. How not to care that laundry isn't in the basket
12. How to let go of my need for neatness

The list could go on.

If needed, take some time to investigate each statement, to determine how far it can take you. Then select the best problem statement. For example, look at Problem #11 on my list above. Instead of solving this problem by changing others' behavior, I may want to consider whether I should change my own expectations and just give up this battle, or get my family to work with me to solve the problem.

Now look at #2. I need to ask myself if making this work fun fits my values, or whether it's more important to me to teach kids that life isn't always fun and sometimes we need to be responsible.

In this way, you can work through each option and decide which *feels right* for you. This process isn't always about analysis and data; often, it's based on gut feel and intuition.

Select one problem statement.

START WITH BROAD WISHING

Push yourself to try all the different types of wishes listed in Chapter Seven, and challenge yourself to come up with 30 different wishes to address your chosen purpose statement. You can even start a list of wishes and add to it over subsequent days and weeks as you work on your issue. Remember to start with "I wish…" and focus on unmet needs, not specific action plans.

By way of example, let's assume we chose to focus on Problem Statement #3: How to teach my kids responsibility. Examples for the laundry issue above include:

- I wish my kids had an inner compass for right and wrong.
- I wish my kids were clear on our expectations.
- I wish my kids took pride in carrying out their responsibilities.
- I wish my kids would own their responsibilities so I don't have to worry about them.

- I wish my family felt like part of a team all helping each other.
- I wish to bribe my kids to put their clothes in the basket.
- I wish to fast-forward 20 years so my kids behave like adults!
- I wish we had started giving our kids chores when they were three years old and actually *wanted* to help.
- Etc.

Keep adding to your list as new wishes occur to you. The most important thing to remember is to not edit yourself—once you think of a wish, just write it down as is and forget about it until you think of another wish.

PULL THEMES FROM YOUR WISHES

Once you have at least 30 wishes, look through your list and identify themes that have emerged. This is your territory to consider for solving the problem.

Examples of themes inherent in my list of wishes above include:

- Internal compass / Feel intrinsic rewards
- Clear communication
- Extrinsic rewards
- Instilling adult behaviors / Ownership of chores
- Etc.

START WITH ONE THEME, CHOOSE AN EXCURSION

- Once you have your list of themes, prioritize items according to what you want to work on and what you think will be most effective in solving your problem.

- For example, to address "extrinsic rewards" for putting clothes in the basket every time, I might choose a "Rewards from Other Arenas" list-building excursion. Forgetting about kids and laundry for a moment, here is a list of rewards in general:

- Money
- Miles
- Toys and presents
- Points
- Stickers
- Old fashioned stamp books
- Medals
- Gift cards
- Gold stars
- Special status
- Mystery rewards /surprises
- Trophy
- Earn privileges

FOLLOW THE SIX-STEP PROCESS FROM CHAPTER NINE TO CREATE NEW IDEAS

Using "money" on this list to inspire an idea, I might create: Jar of dimes in each kid's closet—for every dirty clothes item in their basket they get ten cents on laundry day. After several months, money can be used to do a family activity. And items not in the basket will not be washed.

Again, do your excursions and idea generation over a period of several days or even weeks. Because you are working alone and cannot benefit from the diverse thinking of others, working over a period of time can help you take diverse perspectives, as you spend each day differently and are exposed to a diverse range of experiences.

Continue this step until you have at least 50 ideas. If you can get to 75 or 100—even better! Remember that quality comes from quantity, and your first several ideas will be obvious; more innovative ideas will come out over time if you keep pushing yourself to go further.

SET YOUR CRITERIA

As you start your converging step, think about what must be true of an idea in order for it to be accepted and to actually solve your problem. Make a high-level list. For a problem such as this, you may want to consider criteria like:

- Gets all laundry in all baskets, every time
- Is a solution my kids and family have the skills to execute
- Maintains the peace in our household and prevents arguments
- Is easy enough and motivating enough for our kids to maintain over time

SELECT YOUR BEST SOLUTIONS

Go for three or four options to begin with, so others involved in the solution can weigh in and be part of the solution. This will help them feel motivated to work with whatever system you create at the end.

Only present options to others that you are in favor of personally. You want them to choose one solution they like best—and one you like as well—since everyone must participate in the solution for it to be successful.

ANALYZE ASSISTERS AND RESISTERS OF THE CHOSEN SOLUTIONS

As you look at the top options, it can be helpful to do a brief analysis on issues and factors that will *assist* in accomplishing the goal, as well as issues and factors that will *get in the way of* accomplishing your goal.

"Assisters" can be any factor at all. Using the possible solutions above, assisters might include:

- Professional house cleaning every other week
- Visual jar of money kept in plain sight that reminds everyone of our goals
- A catalog photo of the newest LEGOs® space ship set, put on my son's closet door above the laundry basket as his reward for desired behavior (he loves LEGOs®!)
- Etc.

Once you've identified all your Assisters, list Resisters; in my case they might include:

- My daughter is crazy busy and forgetful and means to do her chores but often doesn't get to them.
- Grandma lets them get away with anything and may collect all the dirty clothes before the kids get a chance.
- Dad doesn't believe in bribes, so we will need to be sure he agrees with the system before we get started.
- Etc.

This quick analysis will help guide you to the best options for your situation—those that consider and incorporate all of the circumstances. It will also make your execution stage easier, because you'll know which factors should be built into your solution, and which factors you'll need to overcome to make your solution work.

SELECT YOUR BEST IDEA AND CREATE A DETAILED ACTION PLAN

Use the who-what-when-where-why-how format. Pay particular attention to the why and the how.

CLEARLY COMMUNICATE YOUR PLAN, EXPECTATIONS AND CONSEQUENCES TO EVERYONE INVOLVED

Go over your solution and make sure everyone who must participate agrees with the plan. Allow others to make some tweaks, so they feel they were part of the solution. Have each person write their name at the bottom of the plan, to indicate they are on board. Even small children can write an "X" or scrawl their name; the fact that they were even asked their opinion at all will make them more motivated to comply with the final plan.

Then be clear about each consequence that will occur if the plan is not followed. They may be simple, natural consequences, such as, "You'll be stinky walking around in wrinkled, stepped-on dirty clothes." Or, you can create other consequences, such as "No screen time on laundry day for anyone who has not complied."

Be sure everyone is clear on consequences! Here is a short anecdote about how effective this approach can really be.

> One of my closest friends, Ann, has a daughter, Ali, who was a very spirited child! Ann worked hard to avoid unnecessary conflicts, so she did some problem solving of

her own and came up with her Action Plan and Consequences list.

After thinking the plan through, Ali and her sister, Sara, sat down with Ann and her husband, and they went through the Action Plan and Consequences together. Everyone seemed satisfied with the plan, and it began to work pretty well, especially for Sara, who was a natural rule-follower.

Ali, however, soon figured out how to work the system. A natural rule-breaker, Ali would go up to the refrigerator, read the rule, carefully move her finger over to the associated consequence and mull it over for a minute. She would then usually decide to break the rule, happily accepting the consequence and creating more work for Ann!

Moral of the story: Make sure your consequences are significant enough to affect the desired behavior, but also acceptable to you. Never choose a consequence that inconveniences you. I learned that the first time I grounded my teenager for a month—a consequence that was highly inconvenient for me because I had to be home too, in order to enforce it!

If you are not working with your children, but instead have adults who must comply with your plan, it can still be helpful to build in consequences—but think them through carefully. If they are natural consequences—such as not getting to work on time if the morning carpooling plan is ignored—adults will accept them readily.

SUMMARY OF CHAPTER NINETEEN – DOING IT ALL YOURSELF

1. You may want to do CPS yourself if you are working on a personal problem you don't want to share, or a business problem that is yours alone, or that others don't have time to address.

2. Follow this process when you do it all yourself:
    - Diverge and converge on your problem statement.
    - Develop broad wishes that address the final problem statement.
    - Pull out Themes or Territories.
    - Work each Territory in turn:
        i. Select an appropriate excursion.
        ii. Follow the six-step process.
        iii. Create a range of new ideas.
    - Build your idea list over time, striving for at least 50 different ideas or solutions.
    - Set criteria and select three to four top ideas.
    - Develop Action Plans and share them with any stakeholders, to get buy-in.
    - Analyze Assisters and Resisters as you make your final idea selection.
    - Communicate your Action Plan clearly, to ensure excellence in execution.

TIPS FOR PERSONAL PROBLEM SOLVING

1. This approach works well regardless of the problem. Just like with any skill, the more you use it, the more skilled you will be.

2. Try it on a variety of different problems—some more functional and others more emotional.

3. Save all your papers and materials so it's easier the second time you do it.

TIPS FOR BUSINESS PROBLEM SOLVING

1. I would strongly encourage anyone in business to try this process. You will be amazed at how quickly and easily you can break through any problem that crosses your desk.

2. Run through the process first with an easy problem like, "How to keep my coffee warm longer at my desk," and work up to more difficult problems, such as, "How to get promoted this year."

3. Get in the habit of thinking about problems in terms of "How to," especially with day-to-day issues. You will instantly turn problems into opportunities and negatives into positives.

CHAPTER TWENTY

CREATING A CULTURE OF INNOVATION

Before we wrap up, it would be helpful to take a quick look at the larger context of innovation and creative problem solving. Any company fully committed to innovation has developed at least two of three Key Elements: the Creative Process, the Creative Person and the Creative Environment.

The Creative Process has been explained thoroughly in this book. We will only briefly touch on the two other key elements within a Culture of Innovation: The People and The Environment.

Here is a diagram of the key elements of innovation:

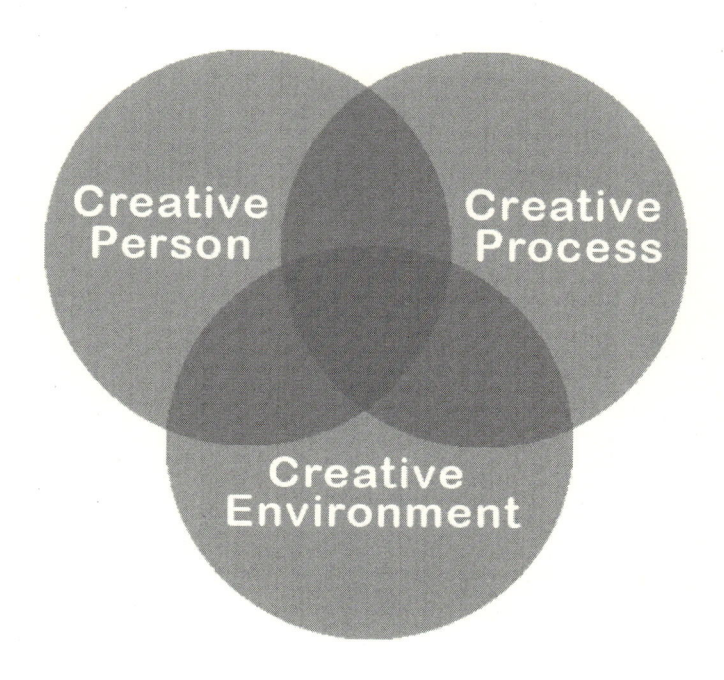

THE CREATIVE PERSON

Several factors affect the Creative Person: creative style preference as measured by the KAI (see Chapter Three), personal habits and blocks—self-editing, internal receptivity and openness to change, for example—and finally, a person's overall health.

1. Personal Habits and Blocks

Some of us were born optimists and some of us pessimists. In my experience, natural-born optimists tend to be more open to new ideas because they have less fear of change.

In addition, the Myers Briggs Personality Type Indicator tells us that some of us were born "Sensors"—the detailed thinkers—and others were born "Intuitors," who are conceptual thinkers. Sensors prefer facts, history and data, and focus on the *past* in order to learn about the future. Intuitors prefer concepts and ideas and a *future* focus, and tend to have little patience for past analysis.

Because of this future focus, many of the best ideators I've employed over the years have been Intuitors, because it seems to come naturally to them. Sensors can also be excellent ideators but will sometimes need a bit more training and practice before new ideas truly flow for them.

Finally, many of us have ingrained habits that are not very useful when it comes to creative problem solving. Self-editing, fear-based interactions and general negativity can all get in the way of developing the creative person that lives inside each of us.

2. Overall Health

This is one of those "unknown assumptions" we discussed in Chapter Five. We all assume everyone is healthy, but health can greatly affect our outlook on life and the way we view future possibilities. Low energy, short attention span, general fatigue, fidgetiness, or an inability to focus are all signs of a problem. If you experience any of these, look for a wide range of possible reasons, because CPS will be the least of your worries!

THE CREATIVE ENVIRONMENT

The last major element contributing to the culture of innovation lies in the environment itself, which is about the physical environment as much as the social and emotional environment. To create a true culture of innovation, your company must value innovation and take *action* to achieve it rather than just giving lip service to the idea. In other words, pay more attention to what management does than what they say.

Several factors contribute to the creative environment: level of trust within a group, a company's appetite for risk, the company attitude or mindset, communications, physical surroundings and, finally, rewards. We will address each in turn.

1. Level of Trust within a Group

This is an extremely important factor when it comes to innovation. Innovation is risky, which is one of the key reasons we insist on using the Greenhouse Thinking™ exercise and enforcing a Greenhouse Environment—it's all about feeling safe enough to put out new ideas.

But trust is a factor long before our meeting starts and long after it's over. If your manager says one thing and does the opposite, nothing you can do as facilitator will make the environment safe when that manager is in attendance.

One technique that can offset a lack of trust in a group is to use online brainstorming. When it's done online, everyone participates at once and all responses are anonymous, so risk is removed from the equation.

2. Company Appetite for Risk

Every individual has a personal idea of what constitutes acceptable versus unacceptable risk, and the same is true for companies. In a company, this is determined by the needs and risk appetite of stockholders, how competitive the market is, the personalities of upper management—particularly the CEO—and whether the company prefers to be an industry leader or follower.

It's easy to call yourself or your company a "renegade," but the true values of a company are determined by where it invests its most precious resources—time, money and labor. If a company calls itself innovative and then fires the first employee whose innovation "fails," a clear message is sent to the entire organization about how risk is truly viewed. In contrast, if a company calls itself innovative and then invests in a new R&D facility and creative spaces, leaders are walking the talk of true innovation.

3. Management Attitude/Mindset

Because companies are made up of people, the attitudes and mindsets of the C-suite will dictate corporate culture. In my experience with Corporate America every company, regardless of size, adopts the attitudes of its CEO. If the CEO is hands-off, most of the managers are also hands-off because that represents the corporation's cultural values. If the CEO is data-driven, the whole organization is data-driven. By the same token, if the CEO is innovative and forward-thinking, so follows the rest of the organization.

4. Communication

As we have seen throughout this book, successful innovation and problem solving require that clear expectations be set around end goals, project objectives, meeting experiences, promised deliverables, etc. Of course, great communication is essential to achieving all this—it doesn't matter how cutting-edge a company culture is if none of the employees know about it. Set clear expectations with employees every day, so you can unleash the creative potential you have in-house.

5. Physical Surroundings

Some environments are more conducive to innovation and problem solving than others. Think about your personal and emotional reaction to a new space that is beautifully designed — your reaction to the atmosphere within a restaurant, for example. Don't you feel differently when you're in a neon-lit fast food restaurant compared to a plush, candlelit steakhouse? When you feel differently you behave differently — and that is the principle at work here when it comes to innovative surroundings.

Creative spaces are bright and fun. If your office is old and tired or your meeting rooms are too small to comfortably accommodate a team of ten, consider securing an outside space for your meeting. Many community rooms are free if you sign up in advance. This bright space off-site will:

- Provide a different environment — compared to your everyday office space — in order to set an expectation for a different kind of work.

- Energize your team because it's light and airy and has natural sunlight.

- Open the team's thinking to different directions because they are not behind the safety of a conference table, but more out in the open in a horseshoe configuration.

- Remove distractions from having email and managers nearby

Creative spaces don't need to be expensive, they just need to be different. Consider a party room at a local science museum, or a meeting room at an art gallery. Jazz clubs and other small concert venues are also fun for daytime meetings, and their managers are usually thrilled to rent the space during daylight hours.

6. Rewards

The last factor contributing to the creative environment is the system of incentives and rewards that relate to innovation. A compensation expert once told me, "Work follows the money, and *only* the money. Change the reward and you'll change behavior."

You can provide direction and assign tasks all you want, but if your employee is being paid for the specific number of customers she brings in (versus the tasks you assign), that is the work she will do first, and with the most enthusiasm. She may or may not ever get to the tasks you assigned.

Truly innovative companies explicitly reward innovation. For example, 3M has had a fabulous financial incentive system among its R&D group for years to foster patent-worthy innovations from any and all scientists. This is a company that actually values innovation rather than just talking about it.

Conversely, you may see a colleague introduce a new product to the market to great fanfare, only to watch him being escorted from the building by Corporate Security when the product fails miserably in the first few months. If something like that happens, no amount of lip service or company communication will ever be able to convince employees that innovation and risk-taking are rewarded.

As I mentioned before, the best measure of a company's values is where it spends time, money and labor resources. If you aren't sure about what your company's values, simply ask around or find an Annual Report to Stockholders, to easily find out where and how resources are actually spent.

SUMMARY OF CHAPTER TWENTY – CREATING A CULTURE OF INNOVATION

1. Three key elements are important for creating a culture in which innovation can thrive: the Creative Process, the Creative Person and the Creative Environment.

2. This book has outlined the Creative Process in great detail.

3. The Creative Person is influenced by:
    - Style of creativity: DaVinci/lateral thinker vs. Edison/linear thinker
    - Attitudes on optimism/pessimism
    - Preference for sensing or intuiting (Myers Briggs)
    - Personal blocks
    - Overall health

4. The Creative Environment is influenced by:
    - Level of group trust
    - Company appetite for risk
    - Upper management attitude and mindset
    - Communication
    - Physical surroundings
    - System of rewards

5. To figure out where a company really stands, follow the flow of resources (time, money and labor). The efforts that receive the greatest investment is what the company truly values.

TIPS FOR PERSONAL PROBLEM SOLVING

1. Identify your Creative Person barriers and determine how to address them.

2. Practice positive thinking habits to change your behavior long term. If you can remove your personal blocks, it will make a world of difference in your skills.

3. Consider taking an assessment of your Creative Style (KAI) or the MBTI Personality Type indicator to get to know yourself better.

4. Create your own innovative environment in which to do your work—a park on a nice day, a sundeck at a casual restaurant, a cozy corner of your bedroom...anywhere that makes you feel different and good.

TIPS FOR BUSINESS PROBLEM SOLVING

1. Culture change takes time. Be patient.

2. Look at the styles of top management to find clues as to how your corporate culture is defined today, and how changeable it really is. If top managers are fairly rigid, hierarchy-driven and focused on the past, your organization may not be very open to making change.

3. Changing rewards will make the biggest difference in changing employee behavior, so if you can, start there first.

4. You have the most control over yourself, so work to break through your personal creative blocks first and you'll accomplish a lot in that first step.

CONCLUSION

SOLVE ANY PROBLEM, ANY TIME

Now you are equipped with all the tools you need to solve any problem that comes into your life, anytime.

Before jumping into big, complex problems, I recommend you practice the processes outlined in this book on some small, low-emotion topics, such as:

- How to keep squirrels off my bird feeder.
- How to make my dog more self-sufficient so he's less work.
- How to get my laundry done in half the time.
- How to get my roommates to share the household chores.

Then you can work your way up to truly difficult problems, such as:

- How to double my income in the next 5 years.
- How to find my perfect life partner.
- How to set my business apart from my competitors.
- How to start up a new high tech company.
- How to overcome U.S. dependence on fossil fuels.

Once you have polished your skills, you will find that every problem is solvable, no matter how difficult or complex.

And then, instead of lamenting, "I HAVE A PROBLEM!" you can happily say, "I *had* a problem but I don't anymore!"

ACKNOWLEDGMENTS

Just as creative problem solving is a team sport, it takes an entire team to write a book.

Special thanks to my daughter Lauren for her consumer wisdom, her hands-on assistance in making this book a reality, and her steadfast partnership every day. Thanks to my mom, Annette for her careful editing, her exceptional command of grammar and her razor-sharp attention to detail. And thank you to my daughter Sam for her creative eye and unique creative vision that has changed my perspective in so many ways. You all made this book possible in your own way.

Thanks to Rachel Maya Fremeth for her ongoing creative inspiration, the illustrations in this book, and the beautiful cover art.

And a special thanks to all the brilliant creative thinkers I've collaborated with over the years, including Fred Meyer, Kim Greene, all of our gifted ConsumerVisionaries™ and KidVisionaries™, Richard Crow, Bill Frost, Sonia Joubert, and many, many more.

INDEX

A

Apples to Apples® Cards, 121

Action Plans, 19, 43, 163-165, 228

Analogies, 30, 35, 111

Analogous Thinking, 97-113

Appeal, Broad, 131, 133, 135

Approximate Thinking, 97-113

Assisters, 225

Assumptions, 46-56

    Busting Assumptions, 49-56

    Known Assumptions, 47-50

    Unknown Assumptions, 30-53

Attendees, 179

Attributes List, 91-92, 126

B

Ballad, 121

Benefit Statements, 153-160

Black Cloud, 213-214

Board Games, 121

Body Language, 205-206

Business Equities, 62, 132-133, 135-136, 234, 236-237

Brainstorm / Brainstorming, 9, 11, 18, 22, 36, 37, 62, 65, 74, 82

Brand Values, 62, 132-133, 135-136, 234, 236-237

Break Times, 202

Broad Appeal, 131, 133, 135

Business Problem Solving, 22-28, 37, 45, 54, 65, 71, 77, 88, 127, 136, 151, 167, 173, 185, 193, 208, 218, 229, 239

C

Cartoon, 98, 103, 112, 121, 140

Champion Process, 12, 148, 150

Character Role Play, 98, 103

Chenille Sticks, 121

Clay, 121

Client, 12-14, 115, 177-178, 194-195, 197, 207

Co-Creation, 12, 143

Collages, 121

Communication Skills, 234-235

Competitors, 25-26, 33, 147, 179

Concept Communication, 169-170

Concepts, 152-165

    Action Plans, 163-165

    Description-Benefit, 158-165

    Insight-Benefit-Reason to Believe, 155-158

    Problem-Solution, 153-155

Consequences, 226-227

Constructive Misunderstanding, 69

Consumers, 12, 131, 133, 152-153, 155, 158, 160, 161-165, 169-170, 172-173, 188, 197

Convergence / Converge, 20, 61, 134, 145, 150, 179, 185, 197, 215, 228

Correcting Clients, 203-206

Costumes, 121

Covey, Steven, 60

CPS, 57-174

CPSI, 12, 18, 19

Creative

    Culture, 230-239

    Environment, 232-237

    People, 231-232

    Problem Solving, 57-174

    Process, 13, 22, 57-174

    Whack Pack®, 245

Creative Education Foundation, 18

Criteria, 129-137

    Concept Communication, 168-170

    Level 1 Strategic Criteria, 129-137

    Level 2 Communication Criteria, 169-170

    Level 3 Practical Criteria, 170-171

    Profitability, 130

    Feasibility, 130

Customers, 131, 132, 138, 152-153, 173, 179, 188, 197, 212

D

Data Excursions, 121-124

DaVinci Style Thinking, 32-37, 238

Daydream, 80, 85-86

Deliverables, 176, 178, 196, 207, 234

Description – Benefit Concept Format, 158-160

Diorama, 121

Diplomat, 214-215

Divergence / Diverge, 18, 20, 61, 179, 185, 228

Do-It-Yourself (DYI), 219-229

Drake, Edwin L., 139

Draw-and-Pass, 108

Drawing, 108, 121

E

Ego, 210

Einstein, Albert, 139

End User, 12, 26, 28, 99, 187, 191

Environment, Creative, 232-237

Environment Photos, 108

Equipment, 180

Equities, Brand or Business, 62, 132-133, 135, 234, 236-237

Excursion Exercises, 89-128

Expectations, 22, 195, 200, 207

Extreme Ideas, 109-111

Evaluation, 129-174

    Champion Process, 12, 148, 150

    Grouping, 142

    Ranking, 142-143

       Rating, 148-149

       Voting, 143-145

Excursions, 79-128

       Exercises, 89-128

             Data Excursions, 121-124

             Draw and Pass, 108

             Environment Photos, 108

             Fantasy, 113-121

             Force Fit, 82

             Get Fired Ideas, 109-111

             Guided Imagery, 118-121

             In-and-Out Listening, 124-125

             LEGOs® Technique, 116-118

             List Building, 91-92, 126

             Picture Cards, 108, 182

             Role Play, 98-104

                    Product, 98-100

                    Target Audience, 100-102

                    Prospect, 100-102

                    Character, 103-104

             Random Objects, 104-107

             Sculpture, 108-109

             SWOTs, 123-124

             Triangle Exercise, 92-95

             Visual Stimulus, 107-109

             Word Association, 95-97

             Worlds Excursion, 111-113

Six-Step Process, 79-88

F

Feasibility, 130

Force-Fit, 82

Formats of Lead Ideas, 152-165

Ford Motor Company, 139

Futuristic Excursions, 113-121

G

Game of Life®, 121

Get-Fired Ideas, 109-111

Greenhouse Environment, 39-45

Greenhouse Thinking™, 38-45

    Benefits, 41-43

    Environment, 39-45

    Technique, 38-45

Group Dynamics, 209-218

Grouping, 142

Group Management Techniques, 209-218

Guided Imagery, 118-121

H

Health, 232

Hypnosis, 81

I

Idea Greenhouse, LLC, 12-14

Imagery, Guided, 118-121

In-and-Out Listening, 124-125

Incubation, 80, 86, 94, 96, 97, 99, 101, 104, 106, 110, 113, 118, 120, 212

Innovation, 20-21, 230-239

Insight, 155-160

Insight-Benefit-Reason to Believe Concepts, 155-158

International Creative Problem Solving Institute, 12, 18, 19

Interpret Aspect Wishing, 68-69

J

Judgement, Personal, 62, 77, 131, 135, 147, 221

K

KAI, 30-34

Key Client, 194-195, 196, 207

Kickoff Meeting, 195-201

Kirton Adaption Innovation / KAI, 30-34

Know-it-All, 215-216

Known Assumptions, 47-50

L

Lateral Thinking, 29-37

Lead Ideas, 152-167

LEGOs® Projective Technique, 116-118

Level 1 Strategic Criteria, 129-137

Level 2 Communication Criteria, 169-170

Level 3 Practical Criteria, 170-171

Likes, 40, 45, 145, 214

Linear Thinking, 29, 35

List Building, 91-92, 126

Logical Rational Excursions, 91-97

Logical Thinking, 29, 35

M

Management, 131, 147, 148, 152, 169, 177, 179-180, 188, 210, 233, 234, 238, 239

Marvel Comics®, 140-141

Meeting Plan, 181

Meeting Room, 180-181

Mental Trip, 126

Metaphors, 35, 80, 97

Meyer, Fred, 11-12, 38

Michigan Savings Bank, 139

Mindset, Positive Thinking, 23-28

Misunderstanding, Constructive, 69

Mouse, 212

N

Needs Assessment, 177-178, 184

Needs, Customer, 62, 132, 135

Negativity, 24, 141, 211, 232

Niche Ideas, 133

Number of Participants, 179

O

On-Demand Ideas, 79-88

Online Brainstorming, 12, 74, 143-144, 190, 233

Opposition Wishing, 69, 71, 72

Order Bias, 145

Osborne, Alex, 9, 12, 18-19

Osborne-Parnes, 19

Open Mindset, 23-28

P

Painting, 121

Paraphrase Wishes, 62, 68

Parnes, Sidney, 9, 12, 19-20

Participants, 179

Passive-Aggressive Master, 211

Personal Habits and Blocks, 231-232

Personal Problem Solving, 22, 27, 36, 44-45, 54, 64, 71, 77, 87, 127, 135, 150, 166, 172, 184, 192, 207, 217, 228, 238, 251

Personal Values, 61, 136, 155, 166, 212, 221

Perspectives, 17, 36, 61, 64, 69, 102, 146, 180, 186, 189-192, 197, 223

Physical Surroundings, 233, 235-236

Picture Cards, 108, 182

Pipe Cleaners, 108, 180

Planning Meeting, 177-185

    Attendees, 179

    Equipment, 180

    Exercises, 181-182

    Meeting Room, 180-181

    Refreshments, 183

Play-Doh®, 120

Pleaser, 213

Poem/Poetry, 121

Positive Thinking, 23-28

Practical Ideas, 81-82

Practicing, 127, 151, 206, 208, 232, 239, 240

Praise, 203-204, 212

Problem-Solution Concept Format, 153-155

Problem Statements, 19, 59-68, 78, 154, 220-221, 228

Process, 57-174

Product Role Play, 98-100

Profitability, 130

Puppeteer, 216

Q

Quantity of Ideas, 17, 197, 200

Quality of Ideas, 185

Quality Check, 168-174

R

Random Objects, 87, 104-106, 126

Ranking, 142-143

Rap Song, 121

Rating, 148-149

Reason to Believe, 155, 157, 166-167, 244, 249

Recording Ideas, 181

Redirection, 203-206

Refreshments, 183

Resisters, 209, 225-228

Rewards, 151, 222-223, 233, 236-239

Risk, 54, 115, 147-148, 152, 169, 170, 173, 184, 208, 233-237

Role Play, 98

    Character, 103-104

    Product, 98-100

    Prospect, 98

    Target Audience, 100-102

Room, Meeting, 180-181, 235-236

Rules of Engagement, 23, 198, 200, 207, 216

S

Saboteur, 210-211

Sacred Cows, 54-55

Scope / Scope Rope, 20, 196

Sculpture Exercise, 108, 120

Selection Process, 129-134, 141-149

Seven Habits of Highly Effective People, 60

Short Story, 121

Six-Step Excursion Process, 82-83, 85-86, 223

Snippets, 152, 165

Solution, 13-14, 17-20, 24-25, 41-46, 51-54, 63, 67-68, 71-75, 90-91, 107, 115, 126, 136, 152-159, 187-193, 224-226

Stakeholders, 178-179, 188, 192-193, 228

Story, Short, 121

Strategic Territory, 66, 68, 73, 77, 79

Supplies, 128, 181-182

Support, 54, 101, 157, 191, 211

Surroundings, Physical, 233, 235-236

SWOTs, 123-124

Synectics, 11

T

Target Audience, 100-102

Team Formation, 179-180, 187-191

Territory, Strategic, 66, 68, 73, 77, 79

Themes, 66, 68, 74-75, 77, 181, 222-223

Thinking Styles, 29-34
- DaVinci Style Thinking, 32-34
- Kirton Adaption Innovation / KAI, 30-32
- Lateral Thinking, 32-34
- Linear Thinking, 32-34
- Thomas Edison Style Thinking, 32-34

Three Lists, 92-95

Time Management, 181-182

Timing of Meeting, 179

Tips and Guidelines, 194-208

Tools, Creative, 89-128

Triangle Exercise, 92-95

Trivial Pursuit® 121

Trust, Group, 233, 238

Types of Wishes, 66-72

    Associations, 69

    Constructive Misunderstanding, 69

    Interpret Aspects, 68-69

    Opposition, 69

    Paraphrase Problem, 68

    Utopian, 70

U

Uniqueness of Idea, 63, 136, 142

Utopian Wishing, 70

V

Values,

    Brand, 62, 132-133, 135-136, 234

    Personal, 61, 136, 155, 166, 212, 221

Van Oeck, Roger, 12

Vision, 138-142, 150-151, 168

Visual Stimulus, 107, 126

Voting, 143-145

W

Warner Brothers, 139

What-So What-Now-What, 121-123

Wishing, 66-72

Word Association Chains, 96-97

Word Association Clusters, 95-96

Worlds Excursion, 111-112, 126, 182

W-W-W-W-W-H (Who, What, When, Where, Why, How), 19, 43, 163-165, 228

Y

Yes But, 39, 138-139